# Personhood
# Revisited

REPRODUCTIVE TECHNOLOGY, BIOETHICS, RELIGION AND THE LAW

## HOWARD W. JONES, JR., M.D.

LANGDON STREET PRESS

Langdon Street Press
212 3rd Avenue North, Suite 290
Minneapolis, MN 55401
612.455.2293
www.langdonstreetpress.com

ISBN-13: 978-1-938296-15-4
LCCN: 2012950957

Distributed by Itasca Books

Cover Design by Jenni Wheeler
Typeset by Madge Duffy
Front Cover Image: Microscopic view of developing fertilized eggs in vitro. Even with this technique, it is not possible to identify the species or determine normalcy.

*Printed in the United States of America*

# Personhood Revisited

# Table of Contents

Foreword      *vii*

Preface      *ix*

Acknowledgments      *x*

Introduction      *xi*

Chapter 1    *IVF, Bioethics and Public Policy*      1

Chapter 2    *Society Reacts to the First IVF in America*      11

Chapter 3    *IVF and the Vatican*      17

Chapter 4    *A Second Meeting in Rome*      43

Chapter 5    *The Ethics Committee of the American Fertility Society (AFS)*      65

Chapter 6    *Conjugal Love*      79

Chapter 7    *Personhood*      85

Chapter 8    *The Worldwide Surveillance of In Vitro Fertilization*      105

Chapter 9    *Assisted Reproductive Technology and the Law*      123

Chapter 10    *The Future of IVF*      139

Glossary      148

References      151

About the Author      157

# *Foreword*

There are medical giants who change the world for the better for all of us. But there are few who, like Dr. Howard W. Jones, Jr., continue to do so at the age of 101.

I first met Dr. Howard Jones and his extraordinary wife and partner, the late Dr. Georgeanna Seegar Jones in the 1980s. The Drs. Jones, along with their friend and colleague, Dr. Mason C. Andrews, were responsible for the first in vitro fertilization birth in the United States. Today, thanks to their groundbreaking work at the Norfolk, Virginia-based Howard and Georgeanna Jones Institute for Reproductive Medicine, millions of aspiring parents have had their dreams come true with the birth of more than six million babies!

As Chairman of the Howard and Georgeanna Jones Foundation for Reproductive Medicine for the last decade, and a member of the Board of Directors for nearly 25 years, I feel very fortunate to have had a front row seat to the development of medical techniques that have so successfully and profoundly served humankind. Over these years, I have been continually amazed by the breadth of Dr. Jones' knowledge and by his willingness and ability to share the unmatched professional judgment and personal wisdom he has gained. It has been my privilege to support in some small way the noble purpose, the standards of excellence, and the relentless dedication that have made the Jones Institute a beacon to the entire world.

These are critically important times for the reproductive sciences. We are seeing exciting advances that offer more people than ever the chance to have families. We are also seeing IVF at the center of a highly-charged ethical, moral and increasingly politicized debate about the most basic issues of personhood.

There is no one better positioned to address these issues than Dr. Howard Jones.

While modern medical and social scientists debate the unique challenges and issues at the intersection of medical technology and ethics, Dr. Jones brings unparalleled insight and perspective. The history, research, and views he shares in this volume come from a man who has explored these ethical issues from their earliest days, and from a man who has led the entire profession through them while showing remarkable sensitivity and humanity. Dr. Jones often quotes a former English professor of his at Amherst College who wrote:

> *I shall be telling this with a sigh*
> *Somewhere ages and ages hence:*
> *Two roads diverged in a wood, and I -*
> *I took the one less traveled by*
> *And that has made all the difference.*

I believe that Professor Robert Frost would be proud of the way his student took those words to heart. And I know I am proud to have walked these roads with Dr. Howard Jones for the past 25 years.

Howard P. Milstein, Chairman
Howard and Georgeanna Jones Foundation
for Reproductive Medicine

# *Preface*

Interestingly enough, both Robert Edwards, the leader of the British team that developed clinical IVF, and I myself, as leader of the first American team to successfully develop the method, were first involved in the social issues of IVF in 1971—seven years before the first British IVF birth and ten years before the first American IVF birth. How this happened is detailed in chapter 1.

Herein, personhood has been revisited from the historical, biological, and civic views in contrast to many other views which have emphasized philosophy.

In this book, I have analyzed traditional Roman Catholic doctrines with great humility, and I realize that the application of twenty-first-century thinking could well be succeeded by the thoughts of future generations.

If some of the abbreviations or words are unfamiliar, I have provided a glossary at the end of this book.

HWJJR

# Acknowledgments

I am grateful to the countless couples whose reproductive failure and whose determination to have a child made it necessary for them to turn to IVF.

I think particularly of those couples who participated in the IVF program during the first few years after IVF became a clinical reality, when the expressed opposition was very vocal, indeed. Without their courage, IVF would not have been developed nor spread around the world as quickly as it did.

On a more intimate note, I am very grateful to colleagues who turned the draft pages of this document and greatly improved it by their suggestions. I think particularly of Ray Adelman, Sabine Andrews, Lucinda Veeck Gosden, Roger Gosden, and Bassam Kawwass.

I also wish to acknowledge the skillful help of Jennifer Gehlhar whose copyediting greatly improved the flow of words in this volume.

Finally, I continue to be grateful to my long-standing administrative assistant of more than thirty years, Nancy Garcia, who has once again used her incredible skills in producing and correcting the pages of this book.

Howard W. Jones, Jr., M.D.
Norfolk, Virginia
2012

# Introduction

When did each of us become a person? The question of when personhood is acquired has been debated by mankind for well over two thousand years. Oddly enough, in the early decades of the twenty-first century, the acquisition of personhood is again a lively topic. Personhood is a status acquired during human development that confers protection by society.

Personhood is a civil issue. Just as there is a legal age required to drive a car and to vote, there is a legal time when each human becomes a ward of the state and is protected; i.e., acquires personhood. Through the ages, various stages of development have been considered as milestones for this acquisition. For example, a heartbeat, quickening, brain waves, and viability, among others, have been considered as the events that bestow personhood, and therefore societal protection.

Personhood was an issue encountered during the early days of in vitro fertilization (IVF). There were other non-biological situations involving ethics, bioethics, morality, religion, public policy, and the law. The legal aspect was not concerned with violating existing law but with creating a situation where there was no law.

It fell to the lot of IVF pioneers to be the first to deal with such challenges on a legal and ethical level. Detailed within this book is the story of how the Norfolk, Virginia, IVF program dealt with personhood while at the same time wrestling with the biological issues to make IVF a clinical reality.

# *One*

## *IVF, Bioethics and Public Policy*

*There was born at Johns Hopkins Hospital in Baltimore, Maryland,*
in early 1971, a child who was found to have Down syndrome.
The child also had a complication that sometimes occurs with
this syndrome, namely, an intestinal obstruction due to a congenital anomaly of the gastrointestinal tract. The parents were
advised that in order to save the life of the child an operation would be necessary. The parents, however, refused to give
permission for the operation, citing that since the child was
mentally deficient they felt it would be better if the child did
not survive. The child did in fact die.

This information reached the ears of Eunice Kennedy
Shriver in Washington and she decided, along with the other
members of the Kennedy family, that this would be an opportunity to have a public discussion about the social attitude
toward individuals with mental handicaps.

Eunice Shriver was the sister of President John F. Kennedy
and Mr. Robert (Francis) Kennedy, U.S. attorney general, both
of whom were later assassinated. The other male in the sibship was Senator Edward M. "Ted" Kennedy of Massachusetts.
There was an additional female member of that sibship, Rose

Marie Kennedy, who was mentally handicapped. Eunice Shriver became very active in attempting to prevent individuals with mental handicaps from being ostracized from society. She saw this happening to her sister and, therefore, seized upon the Johns Hopkins Hospital incident in order to have a public meeting to discuss the ethical aspects of treatment for these individuals. It was also decided that at this meeting it would be desirable to discuss another procedure that was being developed and seemed to have strong ethical overtones, and that was IVF. The suggestion to include IVF was almost certainly made by Andre Hellegers, who had been at Hopkins in 1965 as a faculty member in obstetrics while Robert (Bob) Edwards and I were working to develop human IVF. Andre's relation to the Kennedys will be described below. Robert Sargent Shriver, Jr. (husband of Eunice Kennedy), who was organizing the meeting, called Bob Edwards and invited him to attend the meeting, which was to be held October 14, 1971.

Bob Edwards was a biologist working at Cambridge University in the United Kingdom. He was trained as a geneticist using mice, but only after M. C. Chang, working in Worcester, Massachusetts, achieved IVF in the rabbit in 1959 did Bob think the IVF technique could be applied to the human. However, he was unable to obtain adequate human eggs in the United Kingdom; therefore, he made arrangements to go to the Johns Hopkins Hospital in Baltimore during the summer of 1965. He teamed with me, the clinician of the project, to apply IVF to the human. In our 1965 work, it seemed fertilization of a human egg had not been achieved. This was because 1965 conventional wisdom required identification of fertilization through the microscope—specifically, a sperm tail had to be seen in the egg cytoplasm to prove fertilization. In retrospect, looking at photomicrographs in the publications reporting the 1965 work, IVF indeed had been achieved in the laboratory during the summer of 1965. This was because the presence of pronuclei in eggs had been observed in 1965, and this is now considered proof positive of fertilization. Pronuclei contain the genetic material from the egg and from the sperm. Bob returned to the United Kingdom, teamed up with a clinician, Patrick Steptoe, and would finally produce the world's first test tube baby in 1978. For this, he received the Nobel Prize in Medicine in 2010.

Back on that October day in 1971 when Shriver was organizing the human IVF meeting in Washington, Bob had told him he could not make it, as he was committed to attend a meeting in Tokyo. Sargent Shriver had discovered the Tokyo meeting was actually two days later than the meeting in Washington. Therefore, Sargent Shriver called me, knowing that I knew Bob Edwards. Shriver sought my help in persuading Bob to come through Washington on his way to Tokyo to participate in the ethics meeting.

How Sargent Shriver knew that I knew Bob Edwards is really a story within a story, and it is an important story because it tells how things happen in this world. I will relate that later on. I was able to persuade Bob to attend the Washington meeting, and he changed his route to fly directly from London to the Baltimore–Washington Airport, which at that time had Pan American service. I picked him up at the airport and we drove to Washington to attend the meeting, which was held in the Watergate Hotel (before the Watergate was "the" Watergate). Bob did not know exactly what was to happen at the meeting except that he was to describe IVF and defend its ethical status.

When he found out exactly what the situation was, he was concerned. He discovered there was to be a panel moderated by

Roger Mudd, who was then a well-known television personality. The panel consisted of James Watson of DNA fame; Dr. Leon Kass, a conservative professional ethicist; Dr. Paul Ramsey, a conservative theologian from Princeton; Mr. David Daube, a lawyer; and Dr. Anne McLaren, a distinguished reproductive biologist from London.

Bob was concerned about the attitude of this panel, and he asked me if I would participate. So, at the last minute I joined the panel at Bob's request. In his presentation Bob described IVF and then stated that the ethics of IVF had been discussed and approved by leading ethicists and churchmen in the United Kingdom. The other members of the panel were asked to comment and almost to a person they were either absolutely opposed to what Bob was doing or, in the case of Anne McLaren, not opposed but said that Bob should go slowly because a substantial segment of the population was opposed to what he was doing, largely because he was attempting to do what the panel conceived as beyond the bounds of what science should deal with. Jim Watson said that uncorrectable mistakes would be made and that these mistakes were with human beings, and therefore the work should not be done. Leon Kass also emphasized the possibilities of abnormalities. Paul Ramsey, of course, presented the conservative theological point of view that procreation was, indeed, God's work and humans should not be involved.

Leon Kass' remarks were promptly published in 1971 in *The New England Journal of Medicine*. He stated,

> The coming human technologies of human reproduction pose many difficult and important ethical and social problems. A major question concerns the propriety of perfecting these technologies by experiments

on the unborn and the unconceived. Because the new
procedures for in vitro fertilization and laboratory culture of human embryos probably carry a serious risk of
damage to any child so generated, there appears to be
no ethical way to proceed. One cannot ethically choose
for a child the unknown hazards that he must face and
simultaneously choose to give him life in which to face
them. Also, one must be careful to avoid exploiting
the desires and hopes of childless couples. The medical
and scientific communities ought to assume the major
responsibility for scrutinizing and regulating the human use of new technologies emerging from research
into human reproduction.

He further said,

In sum, there is at present no way of finding out in
advance whether or not the viable progeny of the procedures of in vitro fertilization, culture, and transfer of
human embryos will be deformed, sterile, or retarded.
Even if we wished to practice abortion on all the mis-
begotten fetuses, we are not and will not be able to
identify (by amniocentesis or other methods) many if
not most of them. Neither can we count on 'nature' to
abort all of them for us.

Paul Ramsey's extended remarks were in two issues of *The
Journal of the American Medical Association* in 1972. The first
sentence of the article states,

I must judge that in vitro fertilization constitutes
unethical medical experimentation on possible future

human beings, and therefore it is subject to absolute moral prohibition. I ask that my exact language be noted: I said, unethical experimentation on *possible future human beings.* By this, I mean the child-to-be, the "successful" experiments when they come.

There followed several pages attempting to support this view by reasoning that would now be difficult for the twenty-first century reader to follow. We do know now that IVF has produced several million children. Those children have been examined by a number of studies; and as of 2011, according to AA Rimm, AC Katayama, and KP Katayama, it is the current opinion that these children are as normal as any children born to infertile couples.

While these gentlemen were speaking, I scarcely could listen to what they said because I was quite uncertain as to what to say, but when my time came, I really in essence became a character witness for Bob and indicated that here was a scientist who was simply using the techniques that had become available to solve a problem everybody wanted solved, and the good that would result from his work would overcome any of the theoretical objections that might be made. While I was speaking, the thought occurred to me that Bob was somewhat in the position of Galileo and so my punch line had been that I thought Bob was suffering the tribulations of Galileo. I mention this particular aspect of the meeting now because when Bob wrote his recollection of this meeting in the book *A Matter of Life,* he detailed this particular event in Washington in one of the chapters. The only comment he made to what I said was that I compared him to Galileo.

There was another interesting aspect of the meeting in Washington. Bob and I were invited to dinner at Sargent

Shriver's house one evening during the course of the meeting. The Shrivers had a very large dining room with four tables, each seating about ten. As we were about to sit down, I noticed that there was an elderly lady in rather nondescript clothes who was sitting two places from me at the table. I had not run into her in the milling about that goes on during the beverage time prior to sitting down at dinners of this kind. As we were sitting down, Sargent Shriver asked each one of us to announce who we were and where we were from. When it came time for this little lady to say who she was, she simply got up and said, "People call me Mother Teresa." Thus, I had an opportunity to have dinner with Mother Teresa, as well as the other members of the panel and other people from the audience.

As with ethical matters, no decision was made at the meeting, but it was interesting to me that as far as I could judge from the reaction of the audience, as by applause and their attention, it seemed to me that those in favor of IVF, namely Bob and I, got more attention and applause from the audience than those who objected it. And, indeed, it is interesting that as time has gone along I think those in favor of IVF have prevailed and the little indication that occurred at this meeting in 1971 was an indication of what was to be the case.

Incidentally, this meeting on ethics—primarily of the attitude toward Down syndrome, but which included IVF—turned out to be the inaugural meeting of the Kennedy Institute, which was in the process of being founded. It was to be a unit of Georgetown University. In that year, the first president of the foundation, Andre Hellegers, was elected. At the official founding of the Kennedy Institute of Ethics on October 1, 1971, it was announced by the president of Georgetown University, the Rev. Robert J. Henle, S. J., that the university had received a grant of $1.35 million from the Joseph P. Kennedy, Jr., Foundation, whose president was Senator Edward Kennedy and whose executive vice president was Eunice Kennedy Shriver. The Rev. Henle further stated,

> Developments in medicine and biology in recent years have raised numerous ethical questions. Creating of "test tube babies" and cloning—which once were chilling concepts confined to life in Aldous Huxley's *Brave New World*—are now being studied, for example, in The United Kingdom by Dr. Robert G. Edwards at the University of Cambridge. Fertilization of human eggs in vitro and subsequent implantation into a uterus is already foreseen.
>
> Genetic engineering on human cells, whether and how much to prolong a dying patient's life, organ transplants and possible genetic abortions when tests show fetuses to have some severe genetic effect are other areas of concern.

While the president of the university voiced this sentiment, the thoughts surely were of Andre Hellegers, who shared the podium with President Henley and Eunice Shriver at the ceremony announcing the opening of the Kennedy Institute of Ethics. As will be described in more detail shortly, Andre Hellegers was exposed to the experiments of Robert Edwards when they were both at Johns Hopkins in 1965 while Edwards and I were in the process of developing a program for in vitro fertilization.

Later observers pointed out that the founding of the Kennedy Institute of Ethics in 1971 marked the "birth" of the term and concept of "bioethics." IVF was clearly part of the stimulus.

This leads me to the story within the story of how Sargent

Shriver knew that I knew Bob Edwards and how he knew that I might be in a position to persuade Bob to come to the meeting in Washington. Andre Hellegers was born in the Netherlands, went to medical school in Edinburgh, and then came to Hopkins for residency training in 1953. He stayed on the staff at Hopkins after his residency training and went with Paul Bruns, a colleague at Hopkins, to Georgetown University in 1967. Thus, Andre Hellegers was at Hopkins—indeed, in the same building and on the same floor—while Bob Edwards was at Hopkins in 1965 doing the experimental work on in vitro fertilization, which eventually led to the birth of the first IVF baby.

But how Andre Hellegers got to know the Kennedys is of interest, too. It happened that Andre Hellegers had a brother, Pierre by name, who was mentally retarded, apparently due to anoxia during labor. At Hopkins while Andre Hellegers was there, the chairman of the Department of Pediatrics was Robert Cooke. He was the father of two children who were mentally retarded on a congenital chromosomal basis. Cooke and Hellegers, therefore, had in common the problem of the societal attitude toward mentally retarded offspring. Furthermore, it needs to be added that Robert Cooke was the medical advisor to the Kennedys during the '60s and '70s in Washington. Thus, it was Robert Cooke who introduced Andre Hellegers to the Kennedys and the tie that brought all of them together was this interest in the social attitude toward mentally retarded children.

In 1967 Paul Bruns was invited to be the chairman of Obstetrics and Gynecology at Georgetown, and he brought along Andre Hellegers to work on fetal anoxia as a research subject. Thus, it was a series of chance circumstances that led to the bioethics of IVF being discussed in 1971—long before the clinical use of IVF—as an add-on to a bioethical discussion of the societal attitude toward individuals with Down syndrome. By the same circumstances, IVF was a subject of the first ever meeting of the Kennedy Institute of Ethics.

# *Two*

## *Society Reacts to the First IVF in America*

*While planning a clinical program for IVF in Norfolk, Virginia,* the team soon encountered an issue of public policy. During this planning, it became necessary to involve the hospital because at that time eggs were retrieved by laparoscopy, a procedure that required hospitalization with full hospital facilities. We, therefore, contacted the director of the hospital, Mr. Glenn Mitchell, who had previously been at Johns Hopkins, and was a long-standing friend.

Glenn Mitchell offered us an excess delivery room at the hospital to serve as an egg retrieval room, and an adjacent instrument sterilizing facility that could be converted into a small laboratory. In the fall of 1979, construction began.

Soon after the construction began, I received a telephone call from Glenn Mitchell advising me that since this was a new procedure, under the law, the hospital would be required to apply for what was called a "Certificate of Need." This was a requirement administered by the Virginia State Health Department to prevent duplication of services in hospitals. He said that since there were no other programs like this, it would be a routine matter. It could be applied for by what was called the administrative route, which was a simplified route where objections seemed unlikely; he also said that I would not be required to appear for the application, and that he would handle the matter completely. Therefore, I did not attend the hearing, which occurred in September 1979, when the application was submitted.

However, the hearing was not as simple as he anticipated. The agenda for this hearing apparently appeared in the local newspaper and during the hearing a very large crowd of right-to-lifers assembled to protest what was being done in the hospital. The application was denied, but the hearing officer said that it would be possible for the hospital to reapply for a Certificate of Need for IVF through what was called the public hearing route, and, indeed, the hospital expressed a willingness to apply in this manner.

Before this was done, it occurred to me that it would be important to determine whether the board of the Norfolk General Hospital and the board of the Eastern Virginia Medical School (EVMS) were supportive of our effort to initiate an IVF program. Therefore, following the administrative meeting where the Certificate of Need was denied and before scheduling a second application, I requested to appear before the board of the hospital and the board of the medical school. In each case, I stated that although we were planning to initiate an IVF program, our plans were incomplete and could easily be cancelled if there were any objections on the part of either board to the initiation of the IVF program. There was a unanimous approval of our efforts to begin this program by both boards. In view of this approval, and feeling that our rear was secure, so to speak, we urged the hospital to reapply for a Certificate of Need through the public hearing route. This hearing took

place on Halloween day, October 31, 1979. The hearing was
scheduled to begin at 2:00 p.m.

Unbeknownst to me, it turned out that prior to the hearing a large group of medical students—gathered together by
Newton Miller, who later became an OB/GYN practicing
physician in Norfolk—appeared at the hearing headquarters,
which was held at the Norfolk Public Health Department near
the campus of the medical school. The students essentially occupied all available seats. So, when several busloads of right-to-
lifers arrived to enter the hearing hall with a view of protesting
the granting of the application, there were no vacant seats in
the auditorium. This caused a considerable amount of over-
crowding and congestion. The fire department was on hand
and would not allow people to stand in the corridors, but,
finally a compromise was reached, and some of the medical
students left, leaving some vacant seats for some of the protes-
tors. The hearing was, therefore, delayed in starting. The then
three national television crews—CBS, NBC, and ABC—were
on hand to record the activities of the protest. It was also
widely reported in the national press and *The Ledger-Star*, a
local newspaper in Norfolk, Virginia. The hearing lasted until
about 8:00 p.m. The right-to-lifers were given an opportunity
to present their protest using invited people from out of town.
We were also prepared by inviting Dr. John Biggers, professor of physiology at Harvard, a long-standing friend from
Hopkins; Dr. Roy Parker, president of the American College
of OB/GYN and chairman of the Department of OB/GYN at
Duke University; another long-standing friend, Bishop Heath
Light, bishop of the Episcopal Diocese of Western Virginia; and
Rabbi Lawrence Foreman from a local synagogue. All spoke on
our behalf. The opposition expressed the objection that abnor-
mal children would be born and that we were interfering with

God's work. There were also some frivolous types of objections; for instance, one protestor accused us of performing incest in a test tube, and that we would experiment with combining a human and a monkey.

While there were diverse arguments offered against the IVF program, the theme that ran through many of them had to do with abortion. Several speakers made the point that, as they understood the IVF process, several eggs would be fertilized and several transferred, but actually only one or maybe two sometimes would result in the birth of a child. This meant that those that did not develop were aborted. Therefore, IVF was causing abortion. It turned out that many of the people who were protesting were right-to-life veterans of the campaign against *Roe v. Wade*. Apparently they had lost their platform to a certain extent and found IVF a convenient new platform to sing the song they had been singing for many years about the terrible events of abortion. We were being accused of causing abortion.

The administrations of the school and the hospital supported our applications by their presence. Dr. William Mayer, president of EVMS, was present and supportive, as well as some members of the trustees of the hospital and medical school.

The presiding officer did not render an opinion on that day. In fact, there were several subsidiary hearings subsequent to this, but at the end in February 1980 the Certificate of Need was granted. However, this was not the end of the matter; the objectors appealed to the court to issue an injunction. Following the hearings on this matter, which were quarterbacked by Dr. Mason Andrews, the chairman of the Department OB/GYN at EVMS, the injunction was not granted. We were finally able to begin the IVF treatments in March 1980. It should be mentioned that even with the granting of the Certificate of

Need our concerns about the ethical aspects of things were not entirely laid to rest. For example, from time to time, a picket line would appear in front of the hospital, causing the patients and, indeed, the doctors to cross the picket line in order to carry out the activities.

At the time of the birth of our first baby, Elizabeth Carr, in December 1981, the leader of the opposition, Mr. Charles Dean, paraded in front of the hospital with a sandwich board saying, "see me for the truth," and he was distributing pamphlets describing the terrible things that were being done.

There was residual local opposition for a number of years in the form of protests to the city councils of the municipalities surrounding Norfolk, which had line items in their budgets in support of the medical school. When the medical school was organized, these communities had provided funds in their budgets, on an annual basis, for the general support of the medical school. The opposition attempted to have these line items removed for two or three years in the early '80s. Dr. Mayer and I would appear before the city council in Norfolk and Chesapeake, particularly, on an annual basis and were able to successfully prevent the removal of these line items in support of the medical school.

# *Three*

## *IVF and the Vatican*

*The success of the IVF program at Norfolk in 1981 was the result* of a team effort.

Original IVF team. Front row left to right: Dr. Mason Andrews, Dr. Jairo Garcia, Dr. Howard Jones, Dr. Georgeanna Jones, Dr. Anibal Acosta; Back row left to right: Deborah Perry, Doris Gentilini, Lucinda Veeck, Linda Lynch, Nancy Garcia, Margaret Whitfield.

Dr. Mason Andrews, the departmental chairman, was an enthusiastic supporter who helped greatly with the many administrative problems that arose. Furthermore, he delivered our first IVF baby, Elizabeth Carr, on December 28, 1981.

Dr. Georgeanna Jones, my beloved wife, was a reproductive endocrinologist and lifelong collaborator. Although she was not actively involved in the activities in chapter 1, she was very much involved in the active IVF program and introduced ovarian stimulation with gonadotropins, the technology that has persisted for more than thirty years.

Dr. Anibal Acosta, an Argentinean, had been a fellow with us at Johns Hopkins, but returned to Argentina. He found the political climate there so uncomfortable that he wished to return to the United States. At that time, the Eastern Virginia Medical School was being formed and Dr. Andrews was delighted to invite him to join the faculty, which he did. This was fortunate in many ways, as Dr. Acosta had specialized in andrology. There were very few gynecologists so trained, but andrology was obviously an important part of IVF and this knowledge greatly contributed to our success.

Lucinda Veeck, later Lucinda Veeck Gosden, became our embryologist. It was not possible to find anybody with human embryological experience. There were no such people. Lucinda was trained in laboratory technology and was an experienced cytogeneticist. She self-instructed herself in human embryology and became a distinguished embryologist and published several volumes and atlases about early human embryology.

Dr. Jairo Garcia, who was also a fellow at Johns Hopkins, completed his fellowship and returned to his native Columbia. Like Anibal Acosta, he found the political climate there unsatisfactory and later wrote asking for a faculty position. At the time, the team needed a fellow. Everything fit together.

The support staff was outstanding. The nurses, Doris Gentilini, Margaret Whitfield, and Debbie Perry, worked enthusiastically without regard to standard hours. Linda Lynch and Nancy Garcia, the latter who became my administrative assistant for over thirty years, took care of the many administrative details and patient contacts the program demanded.

Mason Andrews charged me with being responsible for the development of a Division of Reproductive Endocrinology at the new Eastern Virginia Medical School, as well as the IVF program, which was sort of an add-on but became a reality because of the work of this unique staff.

With the birth of Elizabeth Carr in December 1981 and several other normal children in 1982, it became apparent that Norfolk had successfully mastered the IVF technology. Not surprisingly, there were countless requests to receive trainees at all levels. We responded to these to the best of our ability.

We were also deluged with invitations from around the world to attend meetings to explain our technology. One of these invitations to Georgeanna and me in 1983 was from Professor Silvio Bettocchi, who was chairman of the Department of Obstetrics and Gynecology at Bari, Italy. Professor Bettocchi proposed to have a meeting that would consist of most, if not all, of the professors of obstetrics and gynecology in Italy and would have as its objective the possibility of introducing IVF into Italy.

The organizers of the meeting had also invited Monsignor Carlo Caffarra. At that time he was in the Vatican as president of the John Paul II Institute for Studies on Marriage and Family. This was an appointment by the then Pope John Paul II. The organizers of the Bari meeting obviously thought that Monsignor Caffarra should be there because they hoped to get his approval to start an IVF program. However, it did not turn out that way.

He was very opposed to the program. We had many interesting discussions with Monsignor Caffarra in public, and in private as we were having meals together. It turned out that the notion that IVF was objectionable because it caused abortions, as seemed to be the theme of the Halloween Day hearing in Norfolk, was not the case with the Vatican. He said the problem was that IVF was outside the bonds of conjugal love. We were to return to this theme later at a meeting in Vatican City.

At the Bari meeting, Professor Bettocchi requested that we receive a candidate he had in mind to be the embryologist of the program that they hoped to start in Bari. This proved to be Simona Simonetti. Simona came to Norfolk soon after the Bari meeting and began her training with the intention of returning to Bari to start a program there. However, within the first year that Simona was in Norfolk, Professor Bettocchi unexpectedly died. His successor was less enthusiastic about starting an IVF program. This resulted in prolonging Simona's stay in Norfolk to seven years, during which time she became an expert embryologist and helped train many other embryologists at the laboratory.

Also at the Bari meeting, Professor Luigi Carenza, chairman of the Department of Obstetrics and Gynecology at the University of Rome, "La Sapienza," and fellow member of the Society of Pelvic Surgeons, asked us to receive a trainee. We were happy to do this. This trainee was Giulietta Micara, who was with us for a little over a year. We saw her again in Rome at the time of our meeting at the Vatican, which corresponded with the time her program had harvested and fertilized its first human eggs. Professor Carenza had brought Giulietta to the Bari meeting.

In early 1984, Georgeanna, my wife and co-worker, and I each received similar letters postmarked Rio de Janeiro that were written on the letterhead of the Pontifical Academy of Sciences. The letters were signed by Carlos Chagas as president and stated that in the fall of 1984 the academy hoped to have a meeting in the Vatican Garden regarding IVF. The purpose of the letter was to inquire if we would accept an invitation to attend the meeting in the Vatican if we received one. I was not certain that this was a genuine letter, as I had never heard of the Pontifical Academy of Sciences. I wondered if someone was playing a trick on us; therefore, I did not do anything about these letters for a couple of days. The more I thought of it, however, the more it seemed that perhaps there was something to these letters. Carlos Chagas was not an unfamiliar name to any physician who knew that Chagas disease was described by a physician in Rio de Janeiro by the name of Carlos Chagas. Perhaps there was some connection. I, therefore, decided to contact the Catholic chaplain at the DePaul Hospital in Norfolk about this matter. In fact, I called and invited him to come to our home for dinner. At the dinner, we presented him with these letters and inquired whether he thought they were genuine. He became very excited and recognized the pontifical academy for what it was. He explained that the academy had been formulated during Galileo's time to try to prevent a duplication of the Galileo fiasco on the part of the Vatican. The purpose of the academy, as explained by the chaplain, was from time to time to convene a group of so-called experts to discuss scientific developments and have these scientific developments interpreted by the moral theologians of the Vatican. These interpretations would then be made available to His Holiness for suitable action by the pope and by the Church, in general. We, therefore, replied to Carlos Chagas that we would be prepared to accept an invitation; indeed, an invitation did arrive very promptly for a meeting that was to be held in October 1984.

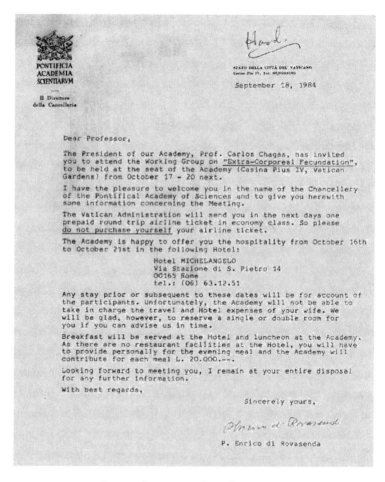

Letter of invitation from the Vatican.

The meeting was held in the Casina Pius IV within the Vatican Gardens. This casina was a beautiful white marble summerhouse that Pius IV built in order to escape the heat of his quarters in the Vatican three hundred yards away. At some time, it had been converted to the headquarters of the Pontifical Academy of Sciences. It turned out that the group being assembled was headed by President Carlos Chagas and consisted of eleven members. There were only three gynecologists: Dr. Rene Frydman of Paris, Georgeanna, and me. The remaining members of the committee were moral theologians or scientists from the Vatican, but there were some from outside, about half and half. Georgeanna and I stayed at the Michelangelo Hotel within the Vatican compound, and I remember that I was the only one without a clerical collar—and Georgeanna for sure was the only woman in the hotel. On the morning of the meetings, we were picked up by the Vatican's personal driver. He drove along the outside wall of the Vatican for half of the commute before entering into the Vatican to drive to Casina Pius IV, where the meetings were held.

Georgeanna and I were oriented by the Monsignor Enrico di Rovasenda, who was in effect the executive director of the casina. He explained that while we were there we would be referred to as "Your Excellency." No one ever used this term.

There were several other points that he made: we would eat lunch in the casina, the appointment as a member of the academy was a lifetime appointment, and in the event of an ecclesiastical procession we would march behind the cardinals and before the bishops. I was particularly impressed by this latter benefit because prior to going to Rome we had had a session with Bishop William Sullivan in Norfolk. He was the bishop of the archdiocese of Richmond, which included Norfolk. The meeting we had with him was a rather stiff meeting in which he expressed great disappointment in what we were doing. We could hardly wait for some conclave that would allow us to get between Bishop Sullivan and the cardinals.

At the organizing meeting, Carlos Chagas explained that the meeting was being recorded and that we were to understand that the walls had no ears, that we were to speak the truth, and that we were to speak to the question of whether in vitro fertilization was licit and consistent with the Catholic doctrine. He also said that we would have an opportunity to read the transcript for accuracy. This transcript was to be published, as all of the deliberations of the academy were said to be, and would be made available to His Holiness as well as to the other members of the Vatican for consideration in formulating instructions for the use of IVF by members of the Church.

There was a very lively discussion for three days. The role of Georgeanna, Rene Frydman, and myself was to describe the IVF process in detail. The group around the table was very interesting. They were highly educated people who could speak several different languages, that is all except Georgeanna and me. We were confined to English. The group would begin talking in one language and then shift to Italian or French, or whatever, and then we would be lost. Therefore, after the first day, Professor Chagas supplied us with a translator who sat between Georgeanna and me. He would quietly translate what was being said into English, and if they lapsed into English he would then translate it into another language, not realizing that he did not need to do that. This translator was none other than Dr. Jerome Lejeune, who happened to be in the Vatican at the time and who was already a member of the academy. In 1959, Dr. Lejeune identified Down syndrome as a chromosomal anomaly—the very first identification of any chromosomal anomaly. He was a faithful Roman who visited the Vatican from time to time and was clearly highly respected, as he would have morning prayers with the pope.

It is worth noting that one of the members of the group was Monsignor Carlo Caffarra, whom we had met in Bari, Italy, previously. Indeed, I suspect that the personnel who were to attend the conference in the Vatican were gotten together by a group including Carlo Caffarra. He remembered his experience in Bari and for this reason, I suspect, we were included in the Vatican group.

The discussion was extremely intellectual. There was a more or less scientific discussion of the process of in vitro fertilization with many, many questions asked by the theologians as we went along. On the last day of the discussion, President Chagas asked each one in turn to say whether they thought IVF should be considered licit or illicit, that is he asked all of the moral theologians present. He did not quiz Georgeanna, Rene Frydman, or me. As he went around the table, each one said that if parishioners came to them and asked if they could have the procedure described, they would have to say they thought the procedure was licit. This was true for everybody except Monsignor Carlo Caffarra. He said he thought it was illicit because it was outside the bonds of conjugal love. We had a very active discussion of exactly what he meant by conjugal love and it turned out that his definition of conjugal love was sexual intercourse. Carlos Chagas made a particular effort to persuade Monsignor Caffarra to change his position and then failing to do that he asked him if he could remain silent, but Caffarra said that he could not. Caffarra pointed out that he had the right ear of the pope. Indeed, this turned out to be the case because in the end the document published by the Vatican, "Instruction *Donum Vitae* on Respect for Human Life in its Origin and on the Dignity of Procreation," called IVF and related procedures "illicit." It was clear that the voice of Monsignor Caffarra overrode the voices of the other theologians that were gathered together to discuss this question.

There were several interesting aspects of our visit within the Vatican. During the first morning we were there, we noticed that the residents of the Vatican kept referring to J. P.

It took us two or three times before we realized that this was the nickname of John Paul II, the pope. We did not think it appropriate to follow suit and we always referred to him as His Holiness.

The Casina Pius IV was located in a fantastic place within the Vatican Garden. There were many coffee breaks, and during the coffee breaks we would go out on an open marble porch, which was immediately adjacent to the outside of the Sistine Chapel. The outside of the chapel was not at all impressive. This was during the era when the chapel was being redone and Monsignor Caffarra offered to take us on a tour of the chapel, but somehow or other during the busy time of the meetings this never did take place.

At no time during the meeting was there a prayer offered. It occurred to us that at the beginning of the meeting it might start with a prayer, but that did not happen. This even applied to the meals. There was never any grace or giving of thanks before a meal. We simply sat down and were served excellent food by nuns who, we were told, "were Polish nuns that came to the Vatican along with J. P." By the way, the food was excellent, in abundance, and accompanied by very nice Italian red wine.

At the opening session of our meeting, we were told that we would be visited by His Holiness on Thursday morning at the Vatican. However, when Thursday morning arrived, this did not prove to be the case. In fact, we were directed to another facility to have our meeting because our regular meeting place was preempted for the signing of a treaty between Chile and Argentina over a border dispute, which the pope had arbitrated. I was absolutely amazed to find that in the twentieth century the pope was still occupied by such secular matters that had been commonplace prior to the Enlightenment. We, therefore, never did see the pope, but received a message through

President Chagas stating his greeting and blessing.

The narrative above was written from memory some years after the meeting. However, in 2011 I retrieved a personal file that contained my own summary of the meeting written in late October 1984. It had been distributed to members of our staff upon return from the meetings. It contains some reiteration of what has been described, but because of its intimacy, it is included below as written in 1984.

> The so-called "working group" on "Extracorporeal Fecundation" consisted of eleven individuals. In addition to the eleven invited people, Professor Carlos Chagas, president of the Pontifical Academy, was present and presided. Professor Chagas is a Brazilian and son of Carlos Chagas, who discovered the spirochete, which causes Chagas disease and is very endemic in certain South American countries. Professor Chagas is perhaps seventy-six years old, very keen. He had an extraordinary ability from time to time to halt the proceedings and summarize, and was able to focus on the important points because during the discussion, there was a tendency for the various participants to stray from the subject. The meeting lasted for three days.

> A word about the participants.

> Professor Baumiller is the Jesuit priest who is responsible for the Genetics Division of the Department of Obstetrics and Gynecology at Georgetown University. He did his genetic training at Hopkins and runs the laboratory for Georgetown University.
> Professor Adriano Bompiani was present only

one day and he is chairman of the Department of Gynecology and Obstetrics at the Catholic University in Italy.

Mons. Carlo Caffarra is president of the Pontifical John Paul II Institute for the Study of Marriage and Family in the Vatican City. We met him in Bari.

Professor Luigi Carenza is chairman of the Department of Obstetrics and Gynecology at the University of Rome and is the chairman of the department who sent Giulietta to Norfolk (the same department in which Giovanni Sadurny works). He was present only one session.

Professor Rene Frydman is well known to the members of the team and he is the director of the in vitro program at the Hospital Beclere in France.

Professor Jerome Lejeune is the discoverer of the fact that Down syndrome was due to G-21 trisomy. He is a well-known, extremely conservative Catholic geneticist who is opposed to aborting G-21 trisomy children. He has testified before the U.S. Senate that life begins with fertilization.

Professor G. Serlupi is the director of the Italian Institute that corresponds to the National Institutes of Health. He is a biochemist by trade, and a very fine gentleman.

The Rev. Padre Jan Visser is a Dutch priest who is a moral theologian in the Vatican.

The last member of the group besides H. W. J. and G. S. J. was Professor Robert J. White, director of Neurosurgery at Case Western Reserve and a Catholic layman, so to speak, but apparently very influential in the inner circles of the Catholic church.

The meeting was held in the Casina Pius IV. This is a small late Renaissance jewel right in the middle of the Vatican Gardens. Vatican City comprises a hundred and three acres, is bound on one side by St. Peters and its appendages, such as the Sistine Chapel and a large new auditorium where the pope has his public audiences, and then the old and new buildings that house the Vatican museums, on top of which is a belvedere where the pope may overlook the city of Rome. The rest of Vatican City is enclosed by walls so that the garden itself is probably of fifty acres, in the center of which stands the Casina Pius IV. It was built by Pope Pius IV as a summerhouse but has, of course, been much modernized in terms of plumbing and electricity. The meeting was held in a large seminar room, with a table that accommodated perhaps twenty seats, within this summerhouse. The building was constructed in 1561. The seminar room had a barrel ceiling with a fresco dating from about that time. The Pontifical Academy of Sciences was founded in 1603 but apparently has recently taken on a new lease of life and its purpose is to inform the Vatican of progress in the mathematical, physical, and natural sciences, and in order to do this organizes plenary sessions and work groups that eventuate in a document transmitted to the pope himself.

A sidelight on all this is that we were informed that as pontifical academicians Georgeanna and I were entitled to be addressed by the title of "Your Excellency" and that in the event of ecclesiastical procession the pontifical academicians would march behind the cardinals and in front of the bishops. We were also informed that this distinction, if that's what it is, is a lifetime designation. We could hardly wait for some conclave that would allow us to get between Bishop Sullivan and the cardinals.

At the first meeting, Professor Chagas, who is a very distinguished and cultured gentleman, said that the meeting would be "free," that "the walls have no ears." He also said that he would like to first discuss the scientific aspects of IVF, later touch on the social and economic implications, and then finally discuss the legal and moral aspects of it; although, the real function of the academy was to produce a document that set forth the current scientific status of the program. He indicated that in order to develop the information we would need to discuss cryopreservation of concepti, whether there were any abnormalities identified within IVF humans, etc., etc. He seemed resolved in the time period in which ensoulment occurs and, in fact, in the subsequent discussions there was no discussion on this topic. It seemed to be assumed by him and by the clergy in attendance that human life began at fertilization.

H. W. J. and G. S. J. were the first called upon to present the state of the art. In view of the fact that in all of the communications there was no mention of any agenda, we had very few slides with us; fortunately, I had brought along the slide of our results by year, the results by trial, and emphasized the inefficiency of human reproduction—specifically pointing out the selection process involved with the oocyte, on one hand, in which there is only one out of twenty oocytes in the ovary available for ovulation at the beginning of puberty, as well as pointing out that maybe as many as three out of four sperm were abnormal in one way or other, and that the union of sperm and egg in normal reproduction results in a pregnancy in any one cycle of about 20 percent.

Professor Frydman then presented their results, also with very few slides because like us he had no idea what the agenda was. One of the special features of his presentation was their experience with the transvesicle and transvaginal routes.

In the general discussion that followed, there was a great deal of interest in knowing whether fertilization in vivo (specifically placing sperm and egg in the uterus) would work. They were surprised to find that it had been tried, even though very few times in our experience, and also Rene Frydman tried it. They were unaware of the fact that Dr. Gary Hodgen (scientific director of the Jones Institute in Norfolk, Virginia) had tried it on some thirty-odd occasions in the monkey without success. Lejeune was particularly anxious to know why this was so, and one of the conclusions, which I am sure will be in the final written document, will be that more research might be expended on this particular process. I inquired if the Academy of Sciences was prepared to make grants in aid but they said that this was outside of their possibility.

There was a good bit of discussion about experimentation on the conceptus. This was particularly relevant because J. P. II, in an address to a previous working party, had spoken about the undesirability of experiments on the conceptus. This provoked a discussion on the definition of "experiment." It was agreed that an experiment, in the sense that was of concern to the pope, implied the destruction by necessity by design during the course of the experiment. It specifically did not include such things as manipulation of the culture medium, for example, which might have as an effect the failure of the concepti to survive. Professor Chagas seemed to prefer the word "observation" or "modification," saying that all these things were acceptable if the intent was to improve the state of the conceptus, even though in carrying out the procedure the ultimate result might be the destruction of the conceptus.

It was pointed out by Professor Chagas that as we went along even though we were hopefully to confine our activities to the scientific aspect of IVF, the moral implications of the work were part of the discussion. At the end of the day, Chagas summed up and said it seemed clear that from the scientific or technical aspect the technique was a viable, acceptable method and that its efficiency would be compared to that of normal reproduction.

The discussion the next day started off with a consideration of freezing and the preserving of concepti. Frydman explained the medical necessity for this saying that they felt it was medically unwise to transfer more than three fertilized eggs and that in order to preserve the concepti for later use they had resorted to cryopreservation of concepti. Interestingly enough, Father Visser said that he felt that the scientist was under no obligation to use "extraordinary means" to preserve the concepti and that he regarded freezing as an "extraordinary means." He likened it to using "extraordinary means" to preserve life at the end of life. The other moral theologians present expressed considerable surprise, or perhaps "horror" is the more appropriate word and the one that Father Visser had adopted. In discussing the matter of freezing, as the discussion went along, it seemed that the moral theologians were expressing concern about freezing not because of freezing per se and not because of preservation per se but because the scientists present had said that the freezing process would inevitably destroy about 50 percent of the concepti. In other words, I thought that from an ethical point of view they seemed to have no concern about preservation per se. In fact, if that were a method or an alternative to destroying concepti, they seemed to be for it. The discussion on freezing which went on for a considerable period of time sort of ended without any clear resolution of what the eventual document from the discussion might say.

The discussion then turned to other technical aspects of IVF, such as the necessity to produce sperm by masturbation. It was interesting that they quoted Pius XII in 1949 as being against artificial insemination because it required masturbation. Much to my surprise, the moral theologians present made the point that no other pope had repeated this and that this question must now be reconsidered and certainly should not be an obstacle to a discussion of in vitro fertilization. Visser further pointed out that the important thing was the dignity of human procreation and that if this required masturbation this must be an act of love to accomplish this particular objective (at lunch time some of the moral theologians said that Visser was really a Dutchman and that the Dutchmen were really "way

out there" on moral issues). Baumiller pointed out
that Artificial Insemination Husband (AIH), which
required masturbation, was quite acceptable morally
as far as he was concerned and was widely practiced in
Catholic hospitals.

There was a discussion of the definition of "dignity." Visser said that the Vatican did not mention dignity as a result of its deliberations and as far as he was
concerned dignity equated with human nature.

The final day of the meeting concerned out and
out ethical issues in spite of the fact that they had been
dragged in during the course of the discussion. The
lead-off man on the final day was Mons. Caffarra, who
was considered by all the Romans present as being
an arch-conservative. Caffarra listed several problems
from his point of view. First was the fact that IVF separated intercourse from fecundation and interposed a
third party in fecundation in that the technician did
the fecundation. Another point was the question of
whether parents have the right to have children. He
said that no human person has the right to have another person. Thirdly, he expressed concern about the
fate of the "spare" concepti. The final point was the
fact that *Humanae Vitae* teaches conjugal love and that
IVF circumvented conjugal love.

There was a great deal of discussion about this
latter point, and it went on and on and on. He was
asked such questions as, "Suppose the technician that
provided the opportunity for the sperm to fertilize the
egg happened to be the husband?" "Why was there an
interposition of a technician and if there was an interposition is this morally wrong?" "Was conjugal love

synonymous with sexual intercourse?" etc., etc.

Baumiller, a Jesuit, said that at the time of
*Humanae Vitae* it was not possible for fecundation to
occur without intercourse but the world had moved
on since then and that it was a time to have a new look
at the problems.

Frydman pointed out that intercourse is not immediately related to fecundation anyway but might be
separated by as much as two or three days and beside
that the husband did not fertilize the egg. He simply
provided sperm for the egg to be fertilized and that
actually the technician was only facilitating the avail-
ability of the egg to the sperm; thus, the technician
did not cause fertilization. Frydman also pointed out
that there were many "technicians" who are involved
in reproduction, such as the obstetrician.

Caffarra was asked whether it was licit for individuals with nervous disorders, as for example paraplegics,
to have children and he answered with an unequivocal
"no." At the end of the discussion, I thought everybody had worked him over pretty good and that the
only point he really could hold on to as a point of
dogma was the matter of equating conjugal love with
sexual intercourse and that sexual intercourse had to
be part of the process. I believe I am summarizing the
attitude of the great majority of the discussants when I
say that there was a general impression that this was an
extremely narrow and old definition and that conjugal
love should indeed surpass this physical relationship in
the human relation of marriage (at lunch Chagas said
that the ultimate decision was going to be very interesting, that Caffarra had the right ear of the pope and

that he himself, Chagas, had the left ear of the pope, and Chagas thought the pope himself was going to be the one who was going to have to make a decision).

After lunch on this same day, Chagas made a statement, a plea, really a very emotional discourse (which I am sorry I didn't have a recording of) in which he said that those who participate in IVF are really applying an act of love of taking an important step to preserve the family, that masturbation was an act of love for this purpose and that the whole IVF program was an attempt to establish responsible parenthood. He pointed out his own infertility problem of seven years and what the birth of a child had meant to him and how it created a new dimension of love. He said IVF is not only a technical question of morality in the philosophical sense but was also a question of charity and that those who were strict in the moral definition were not charitable and he ended up saying he made a plea not to condemn the method on a matter of principle. He said he was not necessarily asking for approval but he was asking for at least silence. He said he was not a man of compromise but a man of conciliation.

Baumiller said that on a pastoral level when couples came to him to ask if it was wrong, he would ask them three questions: (1) Does it harm anyone? (2) Is it being done for a frivolous reason for simple convenience? (3) Is it medically necessary (and if it had already been done, was the outcome good)? If a couple answered these questions in the way that he would anticipate, he would say they had committed no wrong.

The final discussion concerned the method of putting together the document that would result from the conference. All of the discussions were taped and I am not really sure how that was left. I think what will inevitably happen will be that Chagas and probably Lejeune will produce a document to circularize to members of the working group for review. I feel sure that all of this will take weeks, maybe even months, so that if the Vatican—i.e., J. P.—takes any action it will be a considerable period of time.

The working party did not have an audience with the pope. This was said to be quite unusual, as he usually did meet with the working parties. But he had been occupied by diplomats from Argentina and Chile who, in fact, in our seminar room one morning signed a treaty of peace between Argentina and Chile over some islands. The signature of the treaty, of course, would have to be ratified by the two governments but they at least ejected us from our seminar room for the second morning of the discussion. Nevertheless, we had a coffee break with them. I had no idea who they were but there was a very handsome cardinal there speaking Spanish to them so he may have been a cardinal from either one of the countries or maybe he was the arbitrator or conciliator.

The whole experience was really quite unreal and I think we can all be justly proud of the fact that Norfolk really turned out to be the main scientific input at the meeting, supplemented, of course, by Rene Frydman.

On a lighter but no less pleasant side, we had the opportunity to see Giulietta every day and we shared with her the excitement of Friday, October 19, when they were able to get two eggs, both of which sounded a tad immature but nevertheless they were the first eggs that had been secured in the program at the University of Rome. We had a chance to see Giuiletta's laboratory, which is absolutely superb. The operating room is immediately next to the lab but to date they haven't been able to persuade the anesthesiologist to use the room because it doesn't have the necessary anesthetic gadgets in it; so, at the moment, they are working in the main O.R., which is a couple of floors away; but eventually this detail should be ironed out.

Georgeanna and I discussed the meeting on the way home, we were more and more astonished about the position of the Vatican—really that of Caffara—because it seemed to be based on animal rather than human physiology. Thus, immediately on arriving back in Norfolk, a letter was dispatched to Chagas expressing our concerns. These concerns were to be the basis of a second meeting in Rome, as described in a subsequent chapter in this book.

EASTERN VIRGINIA MEDICAL SCHOOL

## THE HOWARD AND GEORGEANNA JONES
## INSTITUTE FOR REPRODUCTIVE MEDICINE

603 MEDICAL TOWER
NORFOLK, VIRGINIA 23507
(804) 628-3370

ANIBAL A. ACOSTA, M.D.
MASON C. ANDREWS, M.D.
JAIRO E. GARCIA, M.D.

October 22, 1984

GEORGEANNA SEEGAR JONES, M.D.
HOWARD W. JONES, JR., M.D.
ZEV ROSENWAKS, M.D.

Professor Carlos Chagas                    CONFIDENTIAL
President
Pontifical Academy of Sciences
Casina Pio IV
Vatican City (Rome)
ITALY

Dear Mr. President:

I must write to tell you how moved and honored we were to have been asked
to be a part of the Scientific Session for the evaluation of in vitro
fertilization and to hear the discussion of the moral issues involved.
The hospitality of the Academy, so warm and gracious, is in keeping with
the beautiful surroundings and elevates the mood and aspirations. I do
hope you will convey our thanks to Father di Rovasenda and the entire staff.
If there is an opportunity to also pay our respects to the Holy Father in an
appropriate way, I would wish that this might also be done.

But dear Mr. President, I must also write my thoughts on the moral considerations.
I was amazed and dismayed to hear the statement of the "Catholic" position of the
moral "opposition." I have attended many meetings where the morality and ethics
were discussed and I know no other Christian sect which would hold to such a
moral tenant. In an area which is so vital to the wholeness of the individual
and therefore of a marriage in which the two individuals are united and therefore
considered as one, such a mechanistic, and in the light of modern knowledge, an
inaccurate viewpoint is unthinkable. It is unjust to burden Catholic couples with
such medieval definitions of conjugal love and pagan philosophy. I can only hope
that dear Monsignor Caffarra who is so dedicated, so bright and so compassionate,
will be able to also see the necessity for re-examining the definition in terms
of modern understandings of "nature."

Mature "conjugal love" which in its narrowest sense is interpreted as sexual
intercourse has as its purpose in "nature" three parts which should be of equal
importance. The importance of each of these aspects changes with the individuals
in the marriage as they age. This change of importance has also occurred as the
world has aged. This is the marvelous and unbelievable beauty of the Christian
faith in the teachings of Christ - they are timeless and applicable equally from
generation to generation. As the world has changed from a primitive wilderness
where the chances of survival were small to a world of teeming cities with "death
control" and the chance of survival great, so has the importance of each of the
"natural" functions of intercourse changed.

We have a system of rewards (enkefalin) our natural morphine which rewards
us by a feeling of "goodness" and thereby trains us in the pathway of
"goodness" if we will permit it. Intercourse evokes this "enkefalin"
secretion. It thereby insures the necessary frequency in the human for
intercourse. But there is also another reward which helps to keep the
family together for child rearing and when age prevents it it still
furnishes without the possibility of reproduction its "natural" function
of solace to the elderly.

Dear Mr. President - as the walls of our meeting room had no ears so this
letter has no eyes. I am not a moral theologist - I am a biologist - I am
a Christian and an ethical person. Again, it was a privilege to know you -
may we meet again.

Love,

Georgeanna and Howard Jones

Letter from Howard and Georgeanna Jones to Carlos Chagas.

Significantly enough, we never received a transcript of the meeting and I suspect that this was purposeful. Furthermore, the proceedings of this particular meeting are not included in the list of publications for the Pontifical Academy under the tenure of di Rovasenda. None of the attendees at the meeting of this working party were ever listed among the members of the academy, except for Lejeune (who already was a member).

There may have been others who were invited but did not attend. We received a routine letter from Chagas thanking us for participating.

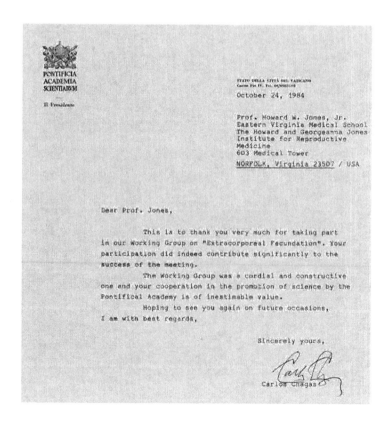

Letter of appreciation from Carlos Chagas.

A few years after the event, I asked my very good Jesuit friend, Father Richard McCormick, if he remembered receiving an invitation. He did but said he refused because he sensed that such working parties were anticipated to support a position already taken and he suspected he might be in disagreement with that position. He therefore declined to attend. The failure to circulate the transcript and the obliteration of a record of the working party from the public documents of the academy are consistent with Father McCormick's view.

In retrospect, it is entirely possible that our meeting with the pope was not cancelled due to his presence at the treaty signing, because I could see that he was not there. The meeting may have been cancelled because he heard that the discussion of the working party was not supporting the position already taken by the magisterium.

The Vatican is by no means free of politics.

There were two consequences of the Vatican meeting. First, it stimulated Georgeanna to write an open letter to the pope. This act in and of itself gave rise to a second meeting on ethics in Rome, and which also will be the topic of a subsequent chapter in this book. Second, it gave rise to the Ethics Committee of the American Fertility Society (AFS), as will also be detailed in a subsequent chapter.

# *Four*

## *A Second Meeting in Rome*

*The 1984 Vatican conference was called together to inform the* Holy Father of the nature of IVF and its offshoots; then the Vatican could issue an instruction in response to inquiries it received about offering IVF and its offshoots to those who apply for its applications. Such an instruction was issued on February 22, 1987. The title was, "Instruction on Respect for Human Life in its Origin and on the Dignity of Procreation Replies to Certain Questions of the Day." The document is often referred to as *Donum Vitae*, the first two words of the Latin version of the document.

The Foreword of *Donum Vitae* sets forth the purpose, and it is as follows:

> The Congregation for the Doctrine of the Faith has been approached by various Episcopal Conferences or individual bishops, by theologians, doctors, and scientists, concerning biomedical techniques which make it possible to intervene in the initial phase of the life of a

human being and in the very processes of procreating and their conformity with the principles of Catholic morality. The present Instruction, which is the result of wide consultation and in particular of a careful evaluation of the declarations made by Episcopates, does not intend to repeat all the Church's teaching on the dignity of human life as it originates and on procreation, but to offer, in the light of the previous teaching of the Magisterium, some specific replies to the main questions being asked in this regard. The exposition is arranged as follows: an introduction will recall the fundamental principles, of an anthropological and moral character, which are necessary for a proper evaluation of the problems and for working out replies to those questions; the first part will have as its subject respect for the human being from the first moment of his or her existence; the second part will deal with the moral questions raised by technical interventions on human procreation; the third part will offer some orientations on the relationships between moral law and civil law in terms of the respect due to human embryos and fetuses and as regards the legitimacy of techniques of artificial procreation.

*Donum Vitae* is a very detailed consideration of IVF and its offshoots, such as donor eggs and donor sperm, the use of surrogacy, and it even approaches other issues of the day, such as homologous insemination in married couples, and, indeed, as an aside, it excludes this as a legitimate procedure, unless it is to facilitate the purpose of intercourse. Thus, it might be used where there was some abnormality of the genitalia, for example, where sperm were not deposited in the vagina, and that circumstance seemed to be licit. For IVF donor eggs and sperm and surrogacy, the instruction is that these are not to be considered because of various reasons, the principal one of which as we have mentioned before is that they are outside the bonds of conjugal love.

Upon reading *Donum Vitae*, Georgeanna was incensed, as this was not at all influenced by the special meeting we had attended in the Vatican. In particular, she thought that *Donum Vitae* was naïve in its understanding of physiology; for example, in one place it states, "it has been demonstrated that from the first instance, the program is fixed as to what this living being will be: a man, this individual man with his characteristic aspects already well determined." This is quite contrary to the conclusion of the Ethics Committee of the American Fertility Society. (See the discussion detailed in chapter 5, The Ethics Committee of the American Fertility Society.) Furthermore, Georgeanna thought that the Vatican was using animal, particularly mammalian, rather than human physiology in regard to intercourse. Animals, in general, have intercourse only when the female is in heat; i.e., when she is ovulating. Thus, in mammals, intercourse is clearly primarily for procreation. In humans, there is no heat—i.e., there is no reliable external sign of ovulation—and, therefore, intercourse must occur at various times during the menstrual cycle so that the unknown ovulatory time will be open to pregnancy. It was not until the early part of the twentieth century that the precise time during the menstrual cycle when ovulation occurs was identified. It is to be noted that there is often considerable variation from cycle to cycle as to exactly when ovulation occurs.

Indeed, the Vatican attitude was puzzling in light of *Humanae Vitae,* an encyclical written by Pope Paul VI and promulgated in 1968. This was promulgated in part to give instruction in regard to the use of birth control. It observed that circumstances often dictate that married couples should limit the number of children and that the sexual act between husband and wife is still worthy, even if it can be foreseen not to result in procreation. Natural family planning—i.e., abstinence during the ovulatory period—is allowed because it took advantage of a "faculty provided by nature." In our 1984 Vatican discussions, it seemed just too much for the Vatican to consider that procreation could be accomplished by other than sexual intercourse. Georgeanna, therefore, wrote an open letter to the pope as follows:

An open letter from Georgeanna Seegar Jones, M.D.

Reply to the Vatican (1987)
"Instruction on Respect for Human Life in its Origin and on the Dignity of Procreation"

I write in response to the Vatican "Instruction on . . . Procreation" as a member of the large majority of the non-Roman Catholic religious community, Christian and Jewish. I write as a practicing gynecologist with a long record of investigative work in reproductive physiology and endocrinology. Perhaps even more importantly, I speak as a wife of 46 years and the mother of three children with successful marriages of 19, 15, and 14 years, respectively.

In 1984, my husband Dr. Howard W. Jones, Jr., and I were invited to the Pontifical Academy of Science at the Vatican for the purpose of explaining the technical and scientific aspects of in vitro fertilization (IVF). We were delighted to participate—as non-Catholics.

We acknowledge the Catholic Church as the largest organization for potential good in the world. We regarded the invitation as an expression of openness and genuine interest in the science of reproduction.

Two years earlier we had participated in an IVF symposium in Bari, Italy, at which the five major Italian universities had joined efforts to gain support for IVF from the Vatican and from the Italian Ministry of Health. There we had had the opportunity to discuss the ethical issues with Monsignor Carlo Caffarra, one of the very conservative theologians of the Vatican, and were amazed to learn that his ethical objection to IVF had nothing to do with abortion, which was the issue often raised in the United States. Rather, the ethical problem, as he saw it, was that IVF "is outside the bonds of conjugal love." My query was, "Do I understand that conjugal love is defined as intercourse?" The answer was, "Yes." My response was then as it is now: "Monsignor Caffarra, in this twentieth century you must change your definition of conjugal love."

Pope Paul VI in the encyclical letter *Humana Vitae* (1968) sought to enlarge the definition of conjugal love as intercourse-for-reproduction by adding to the reproductive function the function of "unity." This is defined by one theologian as "love union" and presumably means love or bonding between couples, but it still makes the conjugal act and conjugal love inseparable. The unitive and procreative functions of the conjugal act are not permitted to be separated ("Instruction," Part 2B, Sec. 4). Therefore, procreating without intercourse is illicit, and intercourse without the possibility of reproduction is illicit. In the Vatican document the definition of conjugal love as intercourse unifies the ethical discussions of all topics related to reproduction. Contraception is prohibited because the act is no longer expressive of the procreative function. Artificial insemination and IVF are prohibited because the procreative function is not by the physical union of the husband and wife.

To me, this reasoning dehumanizes the definition of conjugal love—intercourse, if you will—by insisting that the physical and biological aspects of intercourse must be absolute. It is physiologically possible—and to me ethically permissible—in true conjugal love to separate the function of unity (I call it loving pleasure) from the procreative function, as in the postpartum lactation phase or in the menopause. It is certainly possible physiologically to separate the procreative function from intercourse either by artificial insemination or by IVF. But to me it is never ethical to separate the procreative function between two people from conjugal love. The strongest bonds of conjugal love are those between two loving individuals who are able to make responsible judgments in relation to family formation.

A definition which implies that intercourse is conjugal love, and that the sole function of intercourse is reproduction, does not differentiate between human beings and animals. It is unjust to burden Catholic couples with such a medieval definition. Conjugal love between two human beings should first be a bond of admiration, respect, and mutual interests that produces a lasting spiritual union usually consummated in the physical union of the conjugal act, intercourse.

Reproduction with family formation is surely one of the great pleasures and benefits resulting from the commitment made between two individuals joined in conjugal love and the act of intercourse is physically designed to assure successful culmination of the reproductive process. Because human reproduction is notoriously inefficient, the repetitiveness of the act must be ensured.

This link is made by enkephalin, a natural morphine secreted by the nervous system during intercourse, thereby rewarding us with a feeling of well-being and pleasure, and making intercourse addictive. If the process were otherwise, humanity would not have survived and flourished. This habit formation ensures us that intercourse will occur repetitively enough, in a species without a built-in ovulation signal, so that one intercourse during a month may be successfully timed, and often enough during a year so that one of the successfully timed ovulations will become fertile.

More importantly, in mature conjugal love, the physical act should be inseparable from the spiritual love and respect associated with one special individual in the marriage bond. The union of the pleasurable with the reproductive aspect of the conjugal act provides not only for successful reproduction but also for the stable family formation, which, in human beings as in the primates, is vital to the survival of the young.

The relative importance of these various aspects of intercourse changes as the individuals in a marriage grow older. When age prevents reproduction and when childrearing is completed, intercourse still furnishes—without the possibility of reproduction—its natural function of pleasure. So it is that intercourse from a scientific point of view has not one function but three: (1) reproduction in the early years, (2) a bond to maintain the family formation as childrearing becomes important, and finally, (3) solace to the elderly.

This returns us to the Vatican viewpoint that intercourse is licit only for the purpose of reproduction and that every intercourse must be open to the possibility of reproduction. If one carries this viewpoint to its extreme conclusion, no sterile man or woman should have intercourse. This would include the postmenopausal woman who, presumably with her spouse, would be condemned to abstinence. As this is so obviously impossible and illogical, exceptions have been made to include "unity," for example, the menopause and known medical factors which interrupt fertility—excluding, of course, sterilization procedures. The necessity for the exceptions makes the fallacy of the premise apparent.

If then, the premise—that reproduction without intercourse is illicit or intercourse without reproduction is illicit—is incorrect, Vatican pronouncements against contraception should be reviewed and revised. Although the Vatican has precluded contraception because it induces a condition in which intercourse is not open for reproduction, it has made an exception for rhythm contraception. Such an exception is a scientific fallacy and a contrivance, for it is a well-established fact that intercourse after ovulation has occurred—which is the only effective rhythm method—is never open to reproduction. What is the difference between this form of contraception and taking a pill to ensure a cycle "never open to reproduction?" The answer is that the pill is "unnatural," therefore alien to God's laws. But certainly prohibiting intercourse in a marriage blessed by true conjugal love is unnatural.

The majority opinion of the theologians attending the symposium of the Pontifical Academy to investigate the scientific and ethical aspects of IVF was that basic IVF is an ethical consensus. Monsignor Caffarra was the sole dissenter from this consensus. His final statement was that accepting the IVF procedure as ethical would demand reconsideration of all past pronouncements on the subject of reproduction. The next theologian to speak pointed out that if accepting IVF as ethical meant that the Vatican needed to review and possibly revise all former pronouncements on reproduction, perhaps the time had arrived to do just that.

Those in attendance were to receive the final draft of the scientific and ethical discussions for their review and, if necessary, corrections prior to presentation of the document to the pope for his enlightenment. But no such document was circulated. We therefore conclude that His Holiness is not acquainted with the scientific discussions by the physicians or the ethical judgments of the theologians convened for the express purpose of evaluating the scientific and ethical considerations of IVF. The recent Vatican publication therefore seems to make a mockery of this activity of the Pontifical Academy, which was established during the Renaissance to preclude another Galileo affair.

The Vatican would be well advised, as the twentieth century draws to close, to listen to the collective wisdom of the many dedicated and brilliant ethicists and scientists available within its walls. The Vatican should redefine conjugal love between human beings in terms that emphasize all-encompassing love instead of limiting it to sexual intercourse. The Vatican should realize the scientific factualness—naturalness if you will, God's law as I prefer—of the two-fold function of intercourse, reproduction and pleasure, and the changing importance of the two functions in the lives of two individuals joined in conjugal love.

The pronouncements of natural law were expounded by the early pagan philosophers; in the Judeo-Christian ethic, the laws of nature were regarded as God's laws. We seek to determine the scientific and logical explanation for all of these wonderful and beautiful examples of God's laws. When our investigations indicate either additional functions, such as pleasure in intercourse, or additional therapeutic measures for correction of defects, such as IVF for the treatment of infertility, we should accept these findings as further evidence of God's will for us to be inquisitive and rational. For this is a world of reason that God in His mercy has provided for us. When we know the fact, we must sometimes change our definitions—and even our minds.

The pope certainly did not respond to this letter and probably never saw it. Georgeanna's letter was published in *Fertility News* and was read by Professor Giuseppe Benagiano, who was professor and chairman of the Department of Gynecology and Obstetrics at the University of Rome, "La Sapienza." He was impressed by the letter and on one of his trips to the United States made arrangements to meet with Georgeanna and me in Norfolk, Virginia. We had a wonderful dinner together at the then Omni Hotel where he was staying. As a result of that conversation, and at Professor Benagiano's suggestion, it was planned to hold a second conference in Rome on the general subject of the meaning of sexual intercourse and, indeed, the final title of the meeting when it was held was, "The Evolution of the Meaning of Sexual Intercourse in the Human."

The idea of the meeting was to explore the rationality of the Vatican insisting that procreation arise from sexual intercourse. The presumption was that in the human, intercourse was more than for procreation, particularly, as in the human, signs of ovulation on the part of the woman are not evident and it would not be possible to follow the animal model of having intercourse only when ovulation occurs. Professor Benagiano said he would undertake raising the money for the proposed meeting and, indeed, the meeting did take place despite some delay because it was not easy to find a sponsor. The sponsor turned out to be the Ford Foundation and the background and purpose of the meeting is beautifully set forth in the introduction to the meeting, which was given by Professor Benagiano (at the Palazzo Farnese in Caprarola, Italy, October 19–21, 1992). The proceedings of the meeting were published by the International Institute for the Study of Man under the title, *The Evolution of the Meaning of Sexual Intercourse in the Human.*

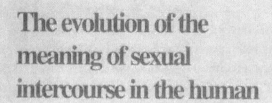

# The evolution of the meaning of sexual intercourse in the human

EDITED BY
**Giuseppe Benagiano**
**Gian Carlo Di Renzo**
**Ermelando V. Cosmi**

ASSOCIATE EDITORS
**James D. Woods**
**Emilio Mordini**

(Tiziano Vecellio: *L'amor sacro e l'amor profano*)

 **International Institute for the Study of Man**

EDITRICE GRAFICA L'ETRURIA - CORTONA

The beautiful Italian book cover of the published documentation
from the second meeting in Rome.

The Introduction by Professor Benagiano is as follows:

It is with great joy that, in the name of the International Scientific Committee, I greet you here today in this beautiful setting, for what we hope shall be a difficult but exciting debate on the true meanings of the single most significant act that two human beings can perform together: the act of beginning a new life.

I am absolutely convinced that believers and non-believers alike should be united in defending and preserving the natural course of this act. This is why I am convinced that—no matter how different and sometimes opposite the views of those present in this room might be—a constructive dialogue is not only possible but mandatory. And this is why we are here today!

This meeting was conceived some three years ago, during discussions with Professor Georgeanna Seegar Jones. At that time we wrote to several people trying to identify both topics and experts.

I must admit that it was not too easy to arrive at a definition of the Agenda for the Meeting, an Agenda that could be agreed upon by all participants as being respectful of everyone's beliefs and ideas, and yet that could allow a frank and open discussion. As a matter of fact we kept modifying the Agenda until very recently.

I also have to admit that it was even more difficult to find someone to agree to provide the funds to make such a discussion possible.

This is why it took us almost three years to convene the workshop: we were looking for sponsors!

As you know, we have obtained a generous grant from the Ford Foundation and I want here to thank with gratitude Mrs. Susan Berresford, the foundation vice president, and Dr. Jose Barzelatto, the director of the foundation's Population Programme, for having so generously made this meeting possible.

The Italian government, through the Honorable Claudio Martelli, the minister of justice, is also sponsoring the meeting and has put at our disposal the beautiful setting of Caprarola. The Honorable Martelli will join us at the end of the meeting, together with Cardinal Fiorenzo Angelini, to close our discussions.

I am supposed to briefly outline for you the scope of our meeting and I shall try to do so.

Central to our debate are the scientific discoveries of the twentieth century, which revealed fundamental differences in sexual behaviour between most higher animals, including non-human primates and the human species. With very few exceptions other female animals only permit mating at the time of ovulation, when they show associated anatomical and behavioural changes.

By contrast, women will permit intercourse through the menstrual cycle, as well as through pregnancy, lactation, and after the menopause. Ovulation in the human is not only not associated with any external signs, but it is so well hidden that it was only in the 1930s that scientists first discovered when, in the menstrual cycle, a woman ovulates.

It is therefore obvious that, for humans, intercourse is much more than simply the act of reproduction, and I believe that it is fair to state that the bonding power of sex within the couple has now been widely recognized by most religious and philosophical schools.

There is however a new aspect to this problem: Recent scientific advances have made it possible for couples to have sex without reproducing, or to reproduce without having had sex.

Our newfound ability to separate the "bonding" from the "reproductive" aspects of sex challenges age-old ideas. For this reason some have been reluctant to even discuss this topic in the fear that it may have disruptive consequences. Scientists, it has been argued, can easily go too far in their zealous manipulation of nature. Let me therefore reassure everyone here that we are not about to steer the meeting in any definite direction, or toward adopting any definite final position.

What I hope we will engage in here during the next two and a half days is the search for truth. As a scientist I am only too (and painfully) aware of Claude Bernard's alleged definition of "scientific truth" as "an imaginary line dividing the error into two parts," the one containing already discovered errors and the one where errors still to be discovered lay hidden! In spite of this, I believe that we must proceed with our search for truth and this, I hope, is what we will be doing. Before mentioning the issue of the continuously changing shape of scientific truth, let me address openly the always present accusation that debating certain arguments means seeding doubt and that, in turn, may have "dangerous consequences." I take strong exception to this idea: it is the honest and public search for truth that must be the basis for every discussion.

Personally, I advocate a fundamental role for scientific research in the construction of bioethical concepts; at the same time, I also strongly believe that it is not up to the scientist as such to draw ethical conclusions from the biological facts he investigates.

A harmonious complementarity of roles requires that science provide data as objective as possible that philosophers and ethicists must accept (although certainly critically)—even when they contradict, as in the case of Galileo, traditional certainties and beliefs—while at the same time it is the task of ethicists to enunciate moral judgments. Their duty is to place the physical facts in a more global perspective, which takes the totality of problems into consideration.

This is not always easy because often we speak different languages, and the difference in language is a continuous source of misunderstanding and friction, when it is not a cause of frank hostility. It is in the nature of this meeting to be open to the danger of failing to communicate because words do mean different things to people involved in different disciplines. We must guard against this trap and patiently look for definitions we can all accept.

Bearing all of this in mind, I hope that we will be able to discuss the true significance of the unique features that the act of intercourse takes in the human. And here comes again the problem of scientific truth. During the course of this meeting our biologist and anthropologist friends will point out the many differences in the process of ovulation and its consequences in the human female when compared to practically all other animal females. This leads to a different pattern of intercourse for the human species.

Our friends will also tell us of recent discoveries, which to a certain extent may at least in part destroy the clear-cut line we have drawn in the past between humans and non-humans.

Even given a certain degree of uncertainty, the question remains unaltered: what is the significance of these differences? Do they imply that the meaning of the act of intercourse is fundamentally different in the human? Does it therefore mean that, in the human, intercourse can be ethically acceptable even when it is stripped of its reproductive meaning, or—on the contrary—no such extrapolation can be drawn and, if so, why?

These and many others are, in my view, the questions that shall pose to one another and then try to at least begin to provide answers.

To make the questions possible we have decided to start the meeting with an overview of the most recent bio-anthropological information.

This will be followed by a review of the evolution of the meaning of the sexual act in the main cultures of our planet. When it comes to culture we tend to be very egocentric, in the sense of often ignoring, or almost, the views of other—equally important—cultural groups.

The meeting has to—by force—focus on the act of intercourse, if we want to carry it to some form of conclusion. We therefore have on purpose left out important topics such as homosexuality.

This does not mean that—whenever you feel that it is necessary—you may not introduce other aspects of the problem.

I hope that in proceeding in this way we will be able to at least define the areas of broad agreement, those where some agreement is possible and those where opposite and irreconcilable positions will continue to exist.

My dream and my hope is to generate enough data and enough interest so that others will enter this field and carry on the search for the true meanings of the act of sexual love.

Before ending, let me thank on your behalf the members of the International Scientific Committee who worked hard to definite the boundaries for this debate and all the members of the Organizing Committee who have spent endless hours trying to make this meeting the success that we all hope it will be.

One final word of thanks to the Associazione per l'Alta Formazione Forum, of which the University of Sapienza of Rome is a member: they are the ones who brought us here in this incredibly beautiful and peaceful setting.

Enjoy the meeting, the discussions and—above all—speak freely: this is why we are here.

Good work!

Giuseppe Benagiano

The discussion by the various presenters of the physiology of reproduction in mammalian species made it clear that *homo sapiens* were different in that there was no external sign of ovulation and, therefore, there had been a disconnect between the frequency of intercourse and ovulation. Thus, in the human, intercourse does occur at times when pregnancy is not possible, as for instance, during pregnancy, amenorrhea, postmenopause, after the uterus has been removed, and at certain times during the normal menstrual cycle.

It was hoped that the participation of Cardinal Angelini, who occupied a position in the Vatican that would be equivalent to the secretary of health, would make it possible for the Vatican to reconsider the reasoning set in *Donum Vitae*. It is significant that *Donum Vitae* was put out by the Vatican under the aegis of the Congregation for the Doctrine of the Faith, the prefect of which was none other than Joseph Cardinal Ratzinger, who, of course, was to become Pope Benedict XVI.

As an interesting aside, it is likely that Carlo Caffara was a principal author of *Donum Vitae*, which as mentioned above was published over the signature of the then Cardinal Ratzinger, now Pope Benedict XVI. It is probably not a coincidence that in the consistory of March 24, 2006, Pope Benedict created Carlo Caffara a cardinal. As such, he was assigned as archbishop of Bologna.

A second consequence of *Donum Vitae* was the reaction of the American Fertility Society Ethics Committee, which, as mentioned previously, had been formed as a result of the Vatican meeting. The Ethics Committee felt it important to respond to *Donum Vitae*, and soon after its publication the Ethics Committee convened in a special meeting to consider the report from the Vatican. The Ethics Committee considered it in detail, wrote a detailed report, and disagreed with the conclusions of *Donum Vitae*. These considerations of the Ethics Committee were approved by the board of the American Fertility Society and published as "Supplement 1" of *Fertility and Sterility* in February 1988. The background of this meeting is put forth in the Foreword to the February 1988 supplement, and is as follows:

> In September 1986, the American Fertility Society issued a report, "Ethical Considerations of the New Reproductive Technologies," (*Fertil Steril* 46: [Suppl. 1], 1986) setting forth the then-held ethical position of the society on the various new reproductive technologies. In 1987, the Congregation for the Doctrine of the Faith issued the "Instruction on the Respect for Human Life in its Origin and on the Dignity of Procreation;" i.e., *Donum Vitae.*
>
> Because of the conflicting conclusions of the two documents, the present Ethics Committee (1986–87) of the American Fertility Society reviewed the guidelines in the light of the Instruction. The succeeding document published as a supplement to the February 1988 issue of *Fertility and Sterility* represents the deliberations of the 1986–87 Ethics Committee. These deliberations were approved by the board of directors of the American Fertility Society at its meeting in September 1987.

After reviewing the AFS guidelines, the committee unanimously reaffirmed the AFS position as published in 1986.

Thus, it seems unlikely that the American Fertility Society, now the American Society for Reproductive Medicine, or the Vatican will change their position. Indeed, the spread of IVF and its offshoots around the world indicates that society in general is prepared to accept the new reproductive technologies; although, of course, there will continue to be a small group who do not wish to benefit by these procedures because of the ideology expressed by the Roman persuasion as well as other persuasions.

The Vatican updated its position on assisted reproductive technology (ART) in September 2008 by issuing "Instruction *Dignitas Personae* on Certain Bioethical Questions."

> The teaching of *Donum Vitae* remains completely valid, both with regard to the principles on which it is based and the moral evaluations which it expresses. However, new biomedical technologies which have been introduced in the critical area of human life and the family have given rise to further questions, in particular in the field of research on human embryos, the use of stem cells for therapeutic purposes, as well as in other areas of experimental medicine.
>
> With regard to the treatment of infertility, new medical techniques must respect three fundamental goods: (a) the right to life and to physical integrity of every human being from conception to natural death; (b) the unity of marriage, which means reciprocal respect for the right within marriage to become a father or mother only together with the other spouse; (c) the specifically human values of sexuality which require "that the procreation of a human person be brought about as the fruit of the conjugal act specific to the love between spouses."
>
> It is true that approximately a third of women who have recourse to artificial procreation succeed in having a baby. It should be recognized, however, that given the proportion between the total number of embryos produced and those eventually born, the number of embryos sacrificed is extremely high. These

losses are accepted by the practitioners of in vitro fertilization as the price to be paid for positive results. In reality, it is deeply disturbing that research in this area aims principally at obtaining better results in terms of the percentage of babies born to women who begin the process, but does not manifest a concrete interest in the right to life of each individual embryo.

It is often objected that the loss of embryos is, in the majority of cases, unintentional or that it happens truly against the will of the parents and physicians. They say that it is a question of risks which are not all that different from those in natural procreation; to seek to generate new life without running any risks would in practice mean doing nothing to transmit it. It is true that not all the losses of embryos in the process of in vitro fertilization have the same relationship to the will of those involved in the procedure. It is also true that in many cases the abandonment, destruction, and loss of embryos are foreseen and willed.

Many other procedures were specifically reviewed: intracytoplasmic sperm injection (ICSI) cryopreservation, selective reduction, preimplantation genetic diagnosis (PGD), contraception, gene therapy, human cloning, stem cell therapy, and hybridization. All were condemned on the basis of willful embryo destruction under the doctrine that ensoulment occurs with fertilization or that the procedure was outside the bonds of conjugal love.

It is clearly unlikely that there will be any change in the attitude of the Vatican in the foreseeable future.

# *Five*

## The Ethics Committee of the
## American Fertility Society (AFS)

*On the plane coming home from the 1984 Vatican meeting in* Rome, I constantly mused on the fact that those involved in the IVF process were certainly involved in a procedure that did not have the approval of a section of the population. The evidence of this, of course, was the experience in the Vatican and the opposition encountered in Norfolk at the beginning of IVF. It furthermore occurred to me, as I thought about this matter, that in the United States at least and, indeed, in most places in the world at that time, IVFers were moving ahead without any particular supervision or guidelines or special laws. Although those involved did have medical degrees and medical licenses, there seemed to be something about reproduction that was special and maybe required special consideration and attention.

As a result of these thoughts, after arriving back in Norfolk, I wrote a letter to Dr. Charles Hammond, the then president of the American Fertility Society. I pointed out to him the notion that I just recorded and suggested to him that the American Fertility Society might wish to consider appointing a committee to draw up guidelines for those involved in the IVF process. As a result of this letter, Dr. Hammond asked me to form a committee and proceed to provide guidelines and directions. The charge to the committee was contained in a letter of November 7, 1984 to me as follows:

> The members of the board and I strongly feel that the American Fertility Society needs to take a leadership position in addressing ethical issues in reproduction providing disseminated knowledge of these positions. Specific issues that we would like considered promptly would include all of the various ramifications of in vitro fertilization (surrogacy, gamete donation, cryopreservation, genetic manipulation, cloning, etc.), specific issues regarding donor insemination—particularly with cryopreservation available—and with multiple pregnancies sired by one individual, sex preselection, patenting medical advances, etc.; and I am sure other issues can be readily thought of.
>
> We would hope that the committee might meet and consider specific questions in a priority they deem appropriate and that they would develop position papers to be submitted to the board of directors and then implemented by the society.

The original committee consisted of eleven individuals: five clinicians, two lawyers, two reproductive biologists, one moral theologian, and one ethicist.

There have been myriads of medical innovations throughout the ages. However, it seems fair to say that IVF and its derivatives generally referred to as assisted reproductive technology (ART), in contrast to all other medical advances, touched a sensitive nerve among a segment of the population that triggered very serious and widespread opposition to its development and use. As described above, it fell to the lot of the pioneers to deal with the bioethical opposition, the issues of public policy, the religious question, and the legal obstacles that detracted from the scientific effort.

However, in the twenty-first century ART is clinically applied throughout the world with only residual opposition. Specifically, ART is bioethically acceptable. It is religiously tolerated by most religious persuasions and it is legally acceptable in practically all countries of the world. It is, therefore, generally speaking, acceptable public policy.

The original committee, which I recommended to the Fertility Society after consultation with appropriate people, was as follows:

Lori B. Andrews, J.D.
Attorney
Project Director in Medical Law
American Bar Foundation
Chicago, Illinois

Celso-Ramon Garcia, M.D.
Obstetrician/Gynecologist
William Shippen, Jr., Professor of Obstetrics
And Gynecology
School of Medicine & Hospital of the
University of Pennsylvania
Philadelphia Pennsylvania

Clifford Grobstein, Ph.D.
Developmental Biologist
Professor of Biological Science and Public
Policy
Science, Technology and Public Affairs
University of California, San Diego
La Jolla, California

Gary D. Hodgen, Ph.D.
Reproductive Biologist
Professor of Obstetrics and Gynecology
Scientific Director
The Jones Institute for Reproductive
Medicine
Eastern Virginia Medical School
Norfolk, Virginia

Howard W. Jones, Jr., M.D.
Professor Emeritus of Gynecology and
Obstetrics
Johns Hopkins University School of Medicine
Professor of Obstetrics and Gynecology
The Jones Institute for Reproductive Medicine
Eastern Virginia Medical School
Norfolk, Virginia

Richard A. McCormick, S.J.
Moral Theologian
Rose F. Kennedy Professor of Christian
Ethics
Kennedy Institute of Ethics
Georgetown University
Washington, D.C.

Richard Marrs, M.D.
Obstetrician/Gynecologist
Associate Professor of Obstetrics and
Gynecology
University of Southern California
Los Angeles, California

C. Alvin Paulson, M.D.
Endocrinologist/Andrologist
Professor of Medicine
University of Washington
Seattle, Washington

John Robertson, J.D.
Attorney/Ethics
Professor of Law
School of Law
University of Texas
Austin, Texas

Edward E. Wallach, M.D.
Obstetrician/Gynecologist
Professor and Chairman, Department of
Gynecology and Obstetrics
Johns Hopkins University School of Medicine
Baltimore, Maryland

LeRoy Walters, Ph.D.
Ethicist
Director, Center for Bioethics
Kennedy Institute of Ethics
Georgetown University
Washington, D.C.

Original Ethics Committee of the American Fertility Society.

In its deliberations, the committee met formally on eight occasions, as follows:

| | |
|---|---|
| Dallas, Texas | February 1-2, 1985 |
| Chicago, Illinois | April 11-19, 1985 |
| Coronado, California | July 29-30, 1985 |
| Chicago, Illinois | October 3-4, 1985 |
| Washington, DC | December 12-14, 1985 |
| New Orleans, Louisiana | February 13-14, 1986 |
| Norfolk, Virginia | March 6-7, 1986 |
| Norfolk, Virginia | April 12-14, 1986 |

Committee meetings on eight occasions.

A member of the committee acted as principal author for each of the chapters. Each chapter was read aloud to the entire committee for comment and discussion. On the basis of such discussion, the chapter was redrafted and the process was repeated until a consensus was reached. A consensus of the majority was reached on each procedure.

The committee consulted experts on highly specialized subjects. For example, the suggested genetic screen for gamete donors was the result of an ad hoc committee chaired by Victor A. McKusick, M.D., professor of medicine at Johns Hopkins University in Baltimore, Maryland.

For the infectious disease screen, the committee relied on "New Guidelines for the Use of Semen for Donor Insemination" (*American Fertility Society*, 1986).

The committee used the terms "artificial insemination–husband" (AIH) and "artificial insemination–donor (AID) to refer to these two well-established procedures.

In its deliberations, the committee accepted certain general principles, as follows:

That the various procedures are offered to the patient(s) only after a medical workup, by accepted medical standards, indicates that the intended procedure(s) will offer a reasonable chance of solving the medical problem.

That the various medical procedures are carried out by trained and experienced personnel in facilities that are properly equipped to offer the sought-after service. For in vitro fertilization (IVF), reference is made to the Minimal Standards statement of the American Fertility Society of January 1984.

That procedures in whatever setting conform to accepted professional and legal standards.

That all clinical experiments and clinical trials, as well as preclinical basic research on human preembryos, have been reviewed by a properly constituted Institutional Review Board and by any other board required by a particular institution and approved by such board(s) before the offering of the service. Procedures under study in clinical experiments are not established medical practice; therefore, general application is premature.

That all other procedures carried out in an institution and subject to review by an Institutional Review Board have been reviewed by a properly constituted Institutional Review Board and by any other board required by that particular institution and approved by such board(s) before the offering of the service by the institution.

That all clinical procedures (including clinical experiments and clinical trials) have been fully explained to all patient participants before the initiation of any procedures. That all patient participants have signed an informed consent.

That, generally speaking, a married heterosexual couple in a stable relationship provides the most appropriate environment for the rearing of a child. However, the committee recognizes that legal marriage does not guarantee a suitable environment and also that the laws of certain states confer on couples living together for various lengths of time all of the legal status provided by a legal marriage. The committee also recognizes that couples or individuals who are not married may, in certain circumstances, assert a moral right to be parents and may be appropriate candidates for medically assisted reproduction.

That requirements of Institutional Review Boards and required reporting of results and procedures are complied with.

In order to avoid confusion, the committee found it necessary to adopt certain definitions for the purposes of this document.

The committee uses the word *couple* to mean a heterosexual couple living together in a stable relationship. In some instances in this report, the context of a recommendation will make clear that the world *couple* also refers to unmarried persons.

A *clinical trial* is considered to be a systematic effort to improve the effectiveness of an existing clinical procedure.

A *clinical experiment* is considered to be an innovative procedure that has a very limited or no historical record of whether any success can be achieved.

A *preembryo* is a product of gametic union from fertilization to the appearance of the embryonic axis. The preembryonic stage is considered to last until fourteen days after fertilization. This definition is not intended to imply a moral evaluation of a preembryo.

The term *egg* is used in a generic sense to mean either an oocyte or an ovum in an unfertilized state.

*Indication* is used as a medical term that designates any sign or symptom of a disease that might lead to a suitable remedy.

After much deliberation the committee finally agreed on a list of subjects, as follows:

- The basis for evaluation of an ethical position
- The constitutional aspects of procreative liberty
- American law and the new reproductive technologies
- Ethics and the new reproductive technologies
- The moral right to reproduce and its limitations
- Ethical consideration of patents in reproductive medicine
- The biologic characteristics of the preembryo
- The moral and legal status of the preembryo
- In vitro fertilization
- Artificial insemination–husband (AIH)
- Artificial insemination–donor (AID)
- Donor sperm in in vitro fertilization
- Donor eggs in in vitro fertilization
- Preembryos from in vitro fertilization for donation
- Uterine lavage for preembryo transfer
- The cryopreservation of sperm

- The cryopreservation of eggs
- The cryopreservation of preembryos
- Research on preembryos; justifications and limitations
- Surrogate gestational mothers: women who gestate a genetically unrelated embryo
- Surrogate mothers
- Quality assurance in reproductive technologies
- Formation of policy for emerging reproductive technologies

When the manuscript was completed, it was forwarded to the American Fertility Society, which passed it on to the board of directors, which approved the content and the document was published as a supplement to *Fertility and Sterility* in September 1986 under the title, "Ethical Considerations of the New Reproductive Technology."

Mr. John Burton, a member of the board of the Jones Institute Foundation, and experienced in public relations, arranged for the material of the report to be presented at a regular meeting of the National Press Club in Washington, D.C., in the fall of 1986. This national exposure gave the publication wide circulation, including editorial notices in many newspapers.

It needs to be emphasized that the recommendations of the committee were simply guidelines, that is to say, they had no legal status, and they were certainly not binding on the various programs. However, it was hoped that there would be enough moral suasion of the American Fertility Society to have the practitioners of IVF follow the recommendations of the Ethics Committee. There were several interesting points about the 1986 recommendations in light of subsequent developments. For example, it was suggested that local institutions have their individual institutional review boards approve the procedures. This, of course, in the twenty-first century is no longer necessary, but, at that time, it indicated that IVF was of an experimental nature. It is also interesting to note some of the details of the recommendations. For example, there had been no suggestion about limiting the number of fertilized eggs that would be transferred. The complication of multiple pregnancies had not been real or appreciated at that time.

During the committee's discussion about when during development personhood was acquired, it became apparent that precise definitions were necessary if we were to communicate accurately with each other. Some of these definitions have been listed in a previous paragraph, but personhood is not listed there. However, it was generally agreed that personhood was that status which was acquired during development at a time when protection by society was expected (first report of the Ethics Committee in *Fertility and Sterility*, 1986).

It was also agreed that personhood as defined equated with the concept of ensoulment in regard to the requirement of societal protection. The soul obviously has other characteristics. This position was agreed upon because it was realized that during the first few days after fertilization it was difficult to know exactly what the developing fertilized egg would yield. Thus, instead of an individual or a person, it could develop into a hydatidiform mole (benign tumor) or a chorioepithelioma (malignant tumor), or there could be twins, or even triplets. Thus, early development was viewed as being biologically uncertain. There was general agreement that the earliest possible point in time for the acquisition of personhood—i.e., protection by society—occurred with the appearance of the primitive streak, which itself guaranteed biologic individuation and eliminated the possibility of a benign or malignant tumor.

On the advice of those who had embryological knowledge, it was agreed that a reasonable time for the primitive streak to appear on average would be fourteen days. This time period represented a remarkable coincidence. In 1978–1979 the Ethics Advisory Board (EAB), appointed by President Jimmy Carter, wrestled with this same problem. Father Richard McCormick, a member of the AFS Ethics Committee, had also been a member of that committee. He recounted that the EAB had difficulty deciding on a particular time and that he himself arbitrarily suggested two weeks (i.e., fourteen days) as a reasonable time. The EAB did not discuss the appearance of the primitive streak so it is a remarkable coincidence that biologically this interval turned out to have some reasonable anatomical marker.

The question then arose as to what name should be applied to the development up until the primitive streak. I personally thought that "proembryo" would be good because both *pro* and *embryo* are Greek in origin; however, the majority thought that pro would be inappropriate because it might be viewed as a substitute for "in favor of." Thus, the hybrid Latin and Greek terminology preembryo was finally selected.

This also turned out to be an interesting coincidence because more or less at the same time interval and without any communication, the Warnock Commission in Great Britain was wrestling with the same problem and seeking a suitable terminology. The late Dr. Anne McLaren was a member of that committee and she later told me that they had considered various names and that they had independently come up with the word "preembryo." The definition of a preembryo was the subject of a publication in 1989 by Jones and Shrader in *Fertility and Sterility*. The Ethics Committee had to consider another troubling detail. The appearance of a primitive streak certainly guarantees biological individuation, but it does not necessarily guarantee normalcy. It is a well-known fact that a measurable percent of early developing fertilized eggs beyond fourteen days nevertheless are abnormal and, indeed, will be aborted because of that abnormality. These abnormalities are largely due to gross chromosomal difficulties, though not entirely.

It is a legitimate question to ask whether these early abortuses because of their abnormality should be considered persons. I suspect that the Orthodox moral theologian would respond in the positive saying that persons can, indeed, be abnormal.

The further question is whether it is desirable to eliminate, if we can, these abnormalities during early development to prevent the birth of the occasional handicapped child, which develops to maturity in spite of the chromosomal abnormality. This, of course, is the whole purpose of preimplantation genetic diagnosis (PGD). In this procedure, a single cell is taken from the developing conceptus at about the eight-cell stage or multiple cells are taken at a later stage and these cells are examined for specific gene defects or for their chromosomal complement. If abnormalities are discovered, that particular conceptus is not transferred and thus the abnormality will be prevented in a newborn child.

In sum, while discussions of this matter may be esoteric and equated with how many angels can dance on the end of a needle, they nevertheless were considered in the document, *Donum Vitae*, which was issued by the Vatican subsequent to the meeting we had in the Vatican described previously.

The science and application of IVF naturally evolved so that the ad hoc Ethics Committee of the American Fertility Society produced two subsequent publications, one in 1990 and one in 1994, each of which were published as supplements to *Fertility and Sterility* in their respective year. After the publication of the 1994 report, the longest existing ad hoc committee of which I have been aware was dissolved and a more permanent ethics committee of the society, now named the American Society for Reproductive Medicine (ASRM), was appointed. This committee, together with the Practice Committee of ASRM, from time to time updated guidelines currently available on the website at www.asrm.com.

Although the committee spent considerable time discussing the chaotic development of the first fourteen days of human development and did not mean to imply any particular moral status in relation to the fourteen days, no member of the committee thought that the discussion had any legal implication. From a legal view, the matter was settled in the minds of the committee by the Supreme Court case in 1973 in *Roe v. Wade*, which held that societal protection during human development was not required until "viability"—i.e., very, very late in pregnancy.

# *Six*

## *Conjugal Love*

*This chapter seeks to understand the origin of the authority for the* adoption of the doctrine that IVF is illicit because it is outside the bonds of conjugal love.

The defining document as applied to IVF seems to be *Donum Vitae*, issued February 22, 1987, and has been cited several times in other chapters. This document is the first external Vatican statement after the clinical application of IVF and was intended to instruct the faithful about the licitness of the clinical application of IVF. *Donum Vitae* confirmed the two principal doctrinal objections to IVF cited by Monsignor Carlo Caffarra at the 1984 Vatican meeting. First, it confirmed that "human life must be respected and protected from the moment of conception." A discussion of this issue (i.e., ensoulment at fertilization) will be found in the following chapter. *Donum vitae* is clear about conjugal love, the topic of this chapter:

> The moral relevance of the link between the meanings
> of the conjugal act and between the goods of marriage,

as well as the unity of the human being and the dignity of its origin, demand that the procreation of a human person be brought about as the fruit of the conjugal act specific to the love between spouses.

It further states:

Conception in vitro is the result of the technical action which presides over fertilization. Such fertilization is neither in fact achieved nor positively willed as the expression and fruit of a specific act of the conjugal union. In homologous IVF and ET (Embryo Transfer), therefore, even if it is considered in the context of "de facto" existing sexual relations, the generation of the human person is objectively deprived of its proper perfection: namely, that of being the result and fruit of a conjugal act.

This was the doctrine orally expressed by Monsignor Caffarra at Bari in 1983 and during the Vatican meeting of 1984. It might well be that Monsignor Caffarra had very direct input into the writing of *Donum Vitae* (1987).

This instruction was reconfirmed on September 8, 2008, with the issuance by the Congregation for the Doctrine of the Faith of *Dignitas Personae*. Therein it states:

The Church moreover holds that it is ethically unacceptable to dissociate procreation from the integrally personal context of the conjugal act.

This, therefore, is the contemporary doctrine of the Church. How and when did this doctrine develop? Conjugal love—i.e., sexual intercourse—had been much discussed in previous Vatican documents, particularly *Gaudium Et Spes* (December 7, 1965). This document was the definitive statement from the second Vatican council (1962–1965) called to review the role of the church in modern society. In discussing family life, it says:

> The biblical Word of God several times urges the betrothed and the married to nourish and develop their wedlock by pure conjugal love and undivided affection.

Further on it states:

> Sons of the Church may not undertake methods of birth control which are found blameworthy by the teaching of the authority of the Church in it's unfolding of the divine law.

It must be remembered that *Gaudium Et Spes* (1965), issued well before the first known IVF success (1978), is the document that updated the role of the Church in modern society and there was a considerable section on contraception. Some delegates to the second Vatican council, as for instance Andre Hellegers, the first president of the Kennedy Institute of Ethics, had hoped there would be some liberalizing of the Vatican attitude toward the use of oral contraceptives that had become available. This did not turn out to be the case, but *Gaudium Et Spes* confirmed the concept that reproduction must be within the bonds of conjugal love.

According to the notes I made immediately after the 1984 Vatican meeting, Carlo Caffarra cited *Humanae Vitae* as a source for the doctrine surrounding conjugal love. *Humanae Vitae* was an encyclical letter by Paul VI issued July 25, 1968. It emphasized, "the regulation of birth." *Humanae Vitae* is significant because it follows *Gaudium Et Spes* by less than three years. This is probably so because, as mentioned previously, there was much vocal lay disappointment that *Gaudium Et Spes* had not allowed the use of the contraceptive pills then coming into widespread use.

It is likely that these protests led Paul VI to circulate *Humanae Vitae* so soon after *Gaudium Et Spes*. *Humanae Vitae* does mention conjugal love but mentions it only once and as an integral part of marriage while holding fast to the much criticized position that only rhythm could be used as a contraceptive method.

However, prior to these documents, Pius XII in an address before the Second World Congress on Human Reproduction and Sterility in Naples on May 19, 1956, referred to the necessity for reproduction to be associated with conjugal love. In 1956, the issue before society was the use of artificial insemination, either by the sperm of the husband or of a donor. At the Naples meeting, Pius XII took occasion to oppose the use of artificial insemination in any form and formulated it in terms of reproduction being necessarily within the scope of conjugal love. Thus, the concept of reproduction within conjugal love had been a point for discussion in relation to artificial insemination and contraception for a number of years prior to 1984 and was probably more discussed within the Vatican than outside. However, it seems very likely that it was Carlo Caffarra who applied this concept to IVF.

Over and above the use of the doctrine of reproduction only by conjugal love in *Donum Vitae* and subsequently in *Dignitas Personae* to condemn IVF, the process of its use is a clear example of how doctrines of this kind have developed throughout the ages. Presumably, with much intramural discussion and outside consultation, the magisterium thus acquires and exerts its moral authority.

# Seven

## Personhood

*The second doctrine that was little discussed but presumably* assumed by most of those present at the 1984 Vatican meeting was the acquisition of personhood with fertilization. Mankind has struggled for over two thousand years to determine when personhood is acquired. This concept remains a hot topic in the twenty-first century, and numerous efforts are being made in the U.S.A. at the state level to declare personhood at fertilization by legislative or ballot means, as will be discussed below.

In this chapter an effort is made to examine the concept of personhood with fertilization from an historical perspective limited to the Western tradition. The word "personhood" as used herein designates a status, the acquisition of which during human intrauterine development or at birth confers upon the conceptus protection by society.

It needs to be noted that the word "personhood" is a product of the nineteenth century, probably mid-nineteenth century. Nevertheless, it will be used to describe the status in question in the materials beginning from early Babylonian and Egyptian works.

## Ancient Babylonia and Egypt

Personhood prior to birth did not seem to be important to some of our earliest civilizations, at least in the documents that are extant. It did not seem to have been considered in Babylonian civilization. Thus, in the Code of Hammurabi (c 1700 B.C.E.) among the laws applying to families, the following references of importance were made.

Law 209 states:

> If a man strike a free-born woman so that she lose her unborn child, he shall pay ten shekels for her loss.

Law 213 states:

> If he strike the maid-servant of a man, and she lose her child, he shall pay two shekels in money.

Note that there is no concern about the stage of the pregnancy and, thus, no modulation of the payment according to the stage of the pregnancy. Although not specified in either of these laws, it may be judged by statements in other laws that the shekels were surely to be paid to the husband of the woman who lost the pregnancy, presumably for the loss of a potential asset of the husband. The Babylonian state seems to have had no stake in the event and no concern about the "unborn child," per se.

Furthermore, there seems to be no mention of personhood among the various Egyptian papyri. However, in the Ebers Papyrus (c 1550 B.C.E.), a medical document listing some seven hundred remedies for various problems, several alternatives were recommended to bring about an abortion. No mention is made about the duration of the pregnancy. Thus, it may be inferred that elective pregnancy termination was quite acceptable to Egyptian society.

## Ancient Greece

Philosophers of ancient Greece, particularly Aristotle, used the word "soul" in relation to embryonic development. However, it is important to understand the Aristotelian concept of soul, because in later Christian literature ensoulment was equated to personhood. This did not seem to be the situation at all in ancient Greece. Aristotle (384–322 B.C.E.) devoted a treatise on the subject of the soul, *De Anima* (Latin). While Aristotle's concept of the soul is quite different from later religious concepts, his view offers a key starting point. Early Christian fathers based some of their dogma on Aristotelian thinking.

Aristotle thought that all living things in order to live required an "activating principle," which he called a *soul*. Aristotle was using the word *soul* in a biological sense to give understanding to something that seemed to be required beyond the physical body for it to live. Aristotle presumed three souls: 1. a vegetative soul required by plants, which bestowed upon them life and reproduction; 2. an animal soul, which bestowed movement and was required by animals in addition to the vegetative soul; and 3. a rational soul acquired at birth only by humans. Thus, animals required the vegetative as well as the animal soul, and humans required all three in sequence.

Of special significance is the Aristotelian concept of when each of these souls is acquired during embryonic development. It is to be noted that Aristotle believed that a vegetative soul was required for life, and, as mentioned above, was required at the very beginning of development. However, the human required an animal soul, as all animals do, early on, but curiously enough, the time of acquisition differed with the sex of the human.

Book VII of *The History of Animals* written 350 B.C.E. by Aristotle states,

> In the case of male children, the first movement usually occurs about the 40th day, but if the child be a female . . . about the 90th day.

This general concept (the point at which there is first movement from a fetus) seems to be what we refer to as "quickening" and this concept is reinforced when one considers that there seems to be no reference in the Aristotelian text as to when the counting begins. If it begins from the time of the missed period rather than the last period, the quickening concept seems extremely likely. The observation with regard to sex and the different times of quickening for each sex has proved, of course, to be inaccurate.

The fact is that the acquisition of a soul recorded by Aristotle had a profound influence for several centuries, not on the nature of the soul, but on the fact that there were different times during pregnancy when the status of the embryo changed.

### Ancient Rome

During several centuries of ancient Rome, the attitude toward personhood may be epitomized by a single quotation from Cicero (106-43 B.C.E.):

> I remember a case which occurred when I was in Asia: how a certain woman of Miletus, who had accepted a bribe from the alternative heirs and procured her own abortion by drugs, was condemned to death: and

rightly, for she had cheated the father of his hopes, his
name of continuity, his family of its support, his house
of an heir, and the Republic of a citizen-to-be.

Notice that there is no mention or concern for the destruction of the conceptus, per se. The concern is because of
the loss of support and hopes of the father—a property loss.
This fits in with the fact that there were no ancient Roman laws
prohibiting abortion.

The situation changes later on in Imperial Rome. It might
be worth quoting Tertullian (155–225 C.E.) because he is
quoted by Pope Benedict XVI, as we will see later. The quote
is:

We are not permitted since murder has been prohibited
to us once and for all even to destroy the fetus in the
womb. It makes no difference whether one destroys
a life that has already been born or one that is in the
process of birth.

## The Christian Era—The Definition of a Christian Soul

The moral status of the conceptus emphasized *soul* beginning
in the early Christian era. In the Christian era, personhood
becomes equated with ensoulment. There is massive, massive
literature on ensoulment, not as defined by Aristotle but as
used in the Christian era. Countless words have been spoken
by clergy and others about the concept of ensoulment. Also,
one can find limitless discussion on ensoulment in the electronic media. It is at least presumptuous to think that anything additive can be said in a short review about ensoulment
in the Christian era. However, personhood as acquired in the
Christian era and the relation of personhood to ensoulment is

so relevant that an attempt must be made to summarize.

If ensoulment, and therefore personhood, occurs with fertilization, it is necessary to agree on an exact definition of fertilization. This is not easy because fertilization is not an event. It is a process. Significantly, there have been some recent ecclesiastical statements that have changed previous language to state that ensoulment is acquired not with fertilization but at the completion of fertilization.

Fertilization can be defined as a process that begins when the sperm contacts the zona pellucida of the egg and ends at the two-cell stage (i.e., approximately twenty-four hours after sperm contact), when, for the first time, each of the two resulting cells has the normal forty-six interphase chromosomes.

The soul is not easy to define. *Merriam-Webster's Collegiate Dictionary*, Eleventh Edition, makes an inclusive statement:

> . . . the immaterial essence, animating principle, or actuating cause of an individual life.

It is infused according to Pope John II at a precise moment. He states in *Evangelium Vitae* (1995):

> . . . scientific and philosophical discussion about the precise moment of the infusion of the spiritual soul . . .

Although early Christian church fathers differed from Aristotle in the definition of the soul, they did adopt the concept of ensoulment during embryonic development (but not at its beginning). This is the pertinent point in these discussions.

The Roman Catholic catechism has dropped the concept of three different kinds of souls and does not view it as an "activating principle" but rather as a "spiritual principle." Thus, the catechism defines the soul as:

> The innermost aspect of humans that which is of greatest value to them that by which they are most especially in God's image: "soul" signifies the spiritual principle in man. [And adds,] the doctrine of faith affirms that the spiritual and the immortal soul is created immediately by God.

It is important to recall the history of the timing of infusion to understand that the current concept of infusion at fertilization, according to current Roman Catholic Church doctrine, is an extremely recent concept in the long sweep of church history. The fact that the doctrine has changed through the ages suggests that the doctrine might be subject to discussion and even further change. While this seems unlikely in the immediate future for the Roman Church, it is relevant to note that other persuasions have done so. For example, in 1990 Miller and Brubaker produced a volume, *Bioethics and the Beginning of Life: An Anabaptist Perspective*, the purpose of which was to discuss these points in light of current scientific knowledge.

St. Augustine (354–430 CE) was a well-educated Roman citizen and prolific writer. He was surely influenced by Aristotle for although he condemned abortion he nevertheless advocated a punishment for abortion related to when the conceptus had received a soul. Augustine followed the Aristotelian concept, stating that males receive a soul at forty days and females at ninety days. It is worth repeating that Augustine's concept of soul was quite different from Aristotle's concept of soul. Augustine regarded the soul as a single entity—i.e., a Christian soul as previously described—but also as mentioned previously, the time of infusion and the variations in time, according to sex, were pure Aristotle.

Gratian, about whose life little seems to be known, was a Benedictine monk who taught in an Abby in Bologna, Italy. He seems to have died in the middle of the twelfth century. Gratian has been cited as a compiler and interpreter of the diverse and conflicting canon laws up to his time. His definitive work is referred to as, "the concord of discordant canons." Gratian cited many examples of previous church fathers who modulated penance for causing abortion, depending on the duration of the pregnancy. Gratian concluded, "he is not a murderer who brings about abortion before the soul enters the body." Interestingly enough, Gratian himself did not seem to indicate a particular time for this to occur. Thus by Gratian's time, the concept of delayed ensoulment seems to have been agreed upon, but note that the sex differences with respect to the time of ensoulment have disappeared.

With the exception of the years 1588–1591, the concept of delayed ensoulment prevailed as church doctrine until the time of Pius IX, the pope with the longest reign, 1846–1878.

The 1588–1591 hiatus was initiated by Pope Sixtus V in 1588 with the papal bull *Effraenatam*, which decreed ex-communication and death for bringing about abortion at any stage of pregnancy. The implication, of course, was that ensoulment had occurred with fertilization.

However, this decree was rescinded three years later (i.e., in 1591) by Pope Gregory XIV, who reinstituted the quickening test, which he determined to be a hundred and sixteen days. Again, there was no reference to sex differences. Thus, delayed ensoulment had been canon law for many centuries until changed by Pope Pius IX in 1869.

Pius IX was pope at a critical time in Vatican history. He was the longest ever reining pope, thirty-two years from

1846–1878. When he became pope, he was temporal ruler of three million citizens of the Papal States, an area as large as the states of Vermont and New Hampshire combined. However, the Papal States were lost to his temporal rule during the unification of Italy by Victor Emanuel and Garibaldi. Beginning in 1866, the civil power of the pope was limited to the present territory of the Vatican, an area slightly more than a hundred acres. There was continuing controversy between the Vatican and Italian state about this matter and others until they were settled in 1929 by the Lateran Treaty, which officially granted civil authority to the pope for the Vatican state as we now know it.

In spite of Pius' loss of civil authority, he issued a record number of encyclicals—thirty-eight in total—almost entirely devoted to sorting out the continual controversy about various theological doctrines. In addition to this, he is well known for convening the 20th Ecumenical Council of the Roman Church, commonly referred to as Vatican I, which was in session from 1869 to 1870 (the council being adjourned because of the outbreak of the Franco–Prussian war). This council confirmed several of Pius' encyclicals and bulls; thus, making them canon law of the church. Included among these were the 1869 bulls in which punishment is outlined for those who commit certain crimes. The highest punishment available to the pope in this era was ex-communication and was prescribed for perpetuators of several acts, including "those seeking to procure (provide or bring about) abortion if the desired effect ensues." The significant aspect of these bulls is that it no longer recognized a period during embryonic development before which ex-communication did not apply. This has generally been interpreted and often cited as the concept that resulted in the modification of canon law to mean that ensoulment, the religious equivalent of personhood, was acquired with fertilization. This matter has been thoroughly reviewed by many, many writers and especially in *The Crime of Abortion in Canon Law*, by Father John Huser.

It is entirely possible that the view expressed in the papal bull of 1869 was influenced by an international concern about induced abortions at any age. This concern was expressed in 1861 by the Parliament of the United Kingdom, which passed the act, Offences Against the Person Act, which outlawed abortion at any stage. In the same year of the papal bull (1869), Canada banned abortion in all provinces. In 1873, the Congress of the United States passed the Comstock Law, which made it a crime to sell, distribute, or own abortion-related products and services.

There is a twenty-first century update to these discussions. With the introduction of oral contraceptives, there were those who held that they were not abortifacients (substances that induce abortion) because pregnancy began with implantation, and as pills operated before implantation oral contraception should be acceptable to the Roman magesterium. However, Pope Benedict XVI in 2010 clarified the view of the Vatican. He said:

> With regard to the embryo in the mother's womb, science itself highlights its autonomy, its capacity for interaction with the mother, the coordination of biological processes, the continuity of development, the growing complexity of the organism. We must say with Tertullian, "The one who will be a man is one already." Thus, there is no reason not to consider him a person from conception.

Below, a twenty-first century evaluation of personhood will be set forth. However, a discussion of ensoulment as a "spiritual principle" might be appropriate at this point. It is to be recalled that such ensoulment has been equated with personhood.

The concept of a "spiritual principle" is a religious statement intended to explain a phenomenon otherwise not explainable. This fits in with what Pope John Paul II wrote in his book, *Crossing the Threshold of Hope* where he states,

> Men turn to various religions to solve mysteries of the human condition.

There can be not the slightest doubt that such religious statements have given great comfort to many people throughout the years.

However, natural reason in the twenty-first century finds it unnecessary to resort to a religious belief to explain fertilization and the subsequent events resulting in the birth of a healthy newborn. It follows that the acquisition of personhood by ensoulment cannot be accepted by natural reasoning of the twenty-first century. However, fertilization will certainly be one of several biological points that will be considered for the establishment of personhood on the basis of a major biological event.

It needs to be added that these comments about soul, defined as a "spiritual principle," do not apply to the use of the word *soul* as otherwise defined. The word *soul* has many, many meanings.

## Secular Concepts of Personhood

As reviewed in previous sections, it was not until the Christian era that attention was devoted to a possible change in the moral status of the intrauterine developing conceptus during development. In addition to the various views of the church fathers, there were several secular ideas put forth.

The lay trigger points to be discussed have been selected on a strictly biological basis to represent major biological events, which have been given significance as indicators of a change in moral status. Interestingly enough, personhood at fertilization has been advocated on primarily biological grounds by Jerome Lejeune, the distinguished French biologist who was to be our interpreter at the 1984 Vatican meeting. Lejeune provided testimony before a U.S. Senate Judiciary sub-committee on April 23–24, 1981, which was considering a law that would have declared personhood with fertilization. This was not adopted but it was a very similar law to the laws being put on ballots in the early twenty-first century. Lejeune stated that life began at conception, but there was not a lengthy biological description.

However, Lejeune's biological reasoning is clearly set forth in his expert testimony at the *Davis Trial* in Tennessee (February 1989). This trial was over the "ownership" of cryopreserved concepti of a divorced couple, the Davises. The issue was the status of the cryopreserved concepti. Using biological terms, Lejeune described the process of fertilization and simply stated that when the genetic material of the male was co-mingled with the genetic material of the female a human being existed. The word "personhood" was not used. There was no discussion of abnormalities at fertilization. Lejeune testified that one could not own a cryopreserved conceptus because one human being could not own another. In the context of this discussion, the outcome of *Davis v. Davis* is irrelevant. The point is that in this case fertilization is presented as an event for the acquisition of personhood. The twenty-first century legislative efforts to declare personhood with fertilization will be discussed below.

Many other biological markers can be considered as evidence of personhood. However, with the exception of fertilization, only those markers which can be externally ascertained will be discussed. These are: heartbeat, quickening, fetal brain waves, and viability.

**Heartbeat**: Rene Laennec (1781–1826) invented the stethoscope in 1816 and published a classical treatis on this discovery in 1819. With Laennec's instrument, the detection of the fetal heart could scarcely be ascertained before about twenty to twenty-four weeks. With modern instruments, the detection would be several weeks before this.

Morale theologians and others who look for some physiological change as an indication of personhood have used the heartbeat as such a sign.

**Quickening**: From ancient times, quickening has been recognized as a sign of life as in the expression, "the quick and the dead." Quickening is usually experienced by women in their first pregnancies during the eighteenth to twentieth weeks. The experience that goes with previous pregnancies usually allows the identification of quickening around fifteen to seventeen weeks. Through history, quickening is likely the sign most often used to indicate a change in status. For example, William Blackstone (1725–1780), an English judge and M.P. (Member of Parliament), in his commentaries on the laws of England states:

> Life . . . begins in contemplation of law as soon as
> an infant is able to stir in the mother's womb. For
> if a woman is quick with child and by a potion, or
> otherwise, killeth it in her womb; or if anyone beat

her, whereby the child dieth in her body, and she is
delivered of a dead child; this though not murder, was
by the ancient law homicide or manslaughter. But at
present it is not looked upon in quite so atrocious a
light, though it remains a very heinous misdemeanor.

There can be little doubt that throughout history quickening has been regarded as the most important sign indicating
a change in moral status.

**Fetal brain waves**: With the development of technology
to identify fetal brain waves, these were advocated as a sign of
personhood. In the *Journal of Medical Ethics* in 1984, Kushner
argued that the cessation of brain waves indicated death so that
the initiation of brain waves can be considered to indicate life.

A simplistic comment is that personhood does not identify life but identifies the stage of life that acquires personhood.
Kushner, however, equated, "life" with personhood.

**Viability**: While viability has been identified as a signal
for personhood from the middle ages, it was only recognized
in civil law in the United States in 1973 at the time of the civil
court decision in *Roe v. Wade*. It will be discussed in detail in a
subsequent section.

## The Laws Against Abortion

In the middle of the nineteenth century, because of propaganda against the use of abortion as a method of contraception
and the mortality associated thereto, several nations passed
several laws against abortion. For example, in 1861 the parliament of the United Kingdom passed the, Offenses Against the
Person Act, which outlawed abortion. In 1869, Canada unified

criminal law in all provinces banning abortion. Due to propaganda efforts joined in by the American Medical Association in the United States in 1873, Congress passed the Comstock Act, which made it a crime to sell, distribute, or own abortion-related products and services or to publish information on how to obtain these. Furthermore, the Comstock Act banned contraception. The law was named for Anthony Comstock, a religious zealot who led the propaganda effort that resulted in the passing of the act. In the Comstock Act, there is no reference to any stage of pregnancy; thus, it could be enforced for any stage.

The present generation may not fully appreciate the consequences of the Comstock Act. It was in force during my early medical career (i.e., from 1931 to 1965), when the Supreme Court in *Griswald v. Connecticut* held that birth control was protected by "a right to privacy."

During these thirty-four years, there was no comment in the medical curriculum at Johns Hopkins, and presumably other medical schools, about elective termination of pregnancy or contraception. However, abortion services were available, though illegal, by practicing physicians; in Baltimore there were two physicians who were known to be available to provide abortion services. This was widely known, but no action was taken against these physicians.

Contraceptive services were provided by a woman physician, Bessie Moses by name, who had offices outside of the Hopkins campus. She gave volunteer courses on contraception at Johns Hopkins and these were well attended, though they began at 5:00 p.m. and lasted until 6:00 p.m. (officially "after operating hours" of the school).

While contraception became legal in 1965, it was not until 1973, a hundred years after the Comstock Act, that *Roe v.*

*Wade* made elective termination of pregnancy legal until fetal viability, as will be described below.

### Reaction Against the Laws Against Abortion

As noted in the preceding section, contraception and contraceptive education and practice became legal only in 1965. In 1973, the Supreme Court in *Roe v. Wade* legalized abortion except for late in pregnancy.

The court decided that the due process clause in the 14th Amendment of the United States Constitution extends to a woman's decision to have an abortion but that right must be balanced against the state's two legitimate interests; i.e., protecting prenatal life and protecting the mother's health. The court resolved this balancing test by limiting abortion to the first two trimesters of pregnancy.

The court later rejected *Roe's* trimester concept while affirming *Roe's* central holding that a person has a right to abortion up until viability. The *Roe* decision defined viability as being "potentially able to live outside the mother's womb albeit with artificial aid." Adding that viability "is usually placed at about seven months (twenty-eight weeks) but may occur earlier even at twenty-four weeks."

Thus, it has been only from the last part of the twentieth century that contraception and its dissemination and induced abortions during the period prior to viability have been legal in the United States.

### The Twenty-first Century

Prior sections of this brief overview have highlighted mankind's struggle to determine when during human embryonic development personhood as defined herein is acquired. In the Western tradition prior to the Christian era, personhood during embryonic development was not a consideration. With the Christian era, personhood at various states of embryonic development did become an issue. Induced abortions during prohibited intervals were considered before ecclesiastical courts. It was not until the mid-nineteenth century with the adoption of the abortion laws that civil courts became involved. How should natural reason in the twenty-first century evaluate personhood?

In the final analysis, personhood is a civil issue. Just as there are certain ages when one is allowed to drive a car or to vote, there must be a certain age when personhood is acquired. In the United States, the current status was established in 1973 by *Roe v. Wade*, as previously described. Specifically, personhood was not acquired until viability; i.e., late in pregnancy.

Nevertheless, there are organizations led by individuals who seek to have the milestone of personhood proclaimed at other triggering points. Fertilization seems to be the process most frequently cited. There have been in the United States at the state level several efforts to bring this about. These efforts have been led by various advocacy organizations; e.g., Personhood U.S.A., Focus on the Family, and perhaps others. There were ballot efforts in Colorado in 2008 and 2010, and in Mississippi in 2011, but these were rejected by substantial margins. Personhood U.S.A. is presently gathering signatures for ballot efforts in Florida, Montana, Ohio, Oregon, as well as Colorado, and perhaps other states.

There was even an effort to introduce a bill into the Congress of the United States in 2012 led by Representative Paul Broun (R-GA), *Sanctity of Human Life Act (H.R. 212)*. This mirrors the Mississippi personhood language. This is certainly a throwback to 1981 when there was a similar effort in Congress, which we have mentioned previously and where

Jerome Lejeune was one of the principal advocates.

Fertilization is the least attractive of the other possible biological events, one of which must be selected to indicate the acquisition of personhood. Fertilization is least attractive because, in simple terms, no one is quite sure what will happen when a sperm meets an egg. Other writers, including philosophers and human embryologists, have advocated fertilization because they say this is THE event in creating a new human individual.

The main problem is that several other things can happen when the sperm meets the egg. These are:

- A benign tumor may form—a hydatidiform mole requires treatment. Are moles persons?
- A malignant tumor may form—a choriocarcinoma is life-threatening and fatal unless treated. Are choriocarcinomas persons?
- Implantation may occur in sites other than the uterus. These ectopic pregnancies are potentially life-threatening and must be removed or otherwise treated. Are ectopic pregnancies persons?
- Twins or more may happen. Is the personhood acquired at fertilization divided so that there is a half person or one-third person?
- An abnormality may occur. There has been little or no discussion by anyone about the fact that the majority of meetings of sperm and egg do not result in a normal human individual. Human reproduction is an extremely inefficient process. Only about one in four, or maybe five, meetings of egg and sperm in normal reproduction results in the birth of a normal individual. In studies of early spontaneous abortions,

it can be shown that two-thirds of the abortions are associated with aneuploidy (abnormal numbers) at the chromosome level. One can speculate that it is extremely likely in the other unexplained abortions that there well may be some mismatch of the genetic combination at the gene level so that there is not adequate genetic information to produce a normal, healthy, live newborn. Do these defective meetings create persons?

Several of the mentioned situations require treatment for the mother, which, if "persons" are really involved and eliminated, could expose the physician to legal liability.

Also, IVF itself could not be an acceptable procedure because it has been considered a cause of abortion of an ensouled person. The so-called abortions in this context refer to the transferred fertilized eggs that do not result in a live birth. Also included as equivalent to abortion, according to various Vatican documents, are those fertilized eggs that are frozen or simply declared as excess and therefore discarded. Furthermore, personhood at fertilization raises a question concerning human evolution.

If personhood applies to humans, when did humans first exist? For example, did Lucy (Australopithecus) acquire personhood? Lucy lived 3.2 million years ago and she walked upright. If not Lucy, when in the evolutionary tree of man did personhood become an issue?

This is scarcely a practical problem in the twenty-first century but surely should be addressed by philosophers, theologians, and others who are concerned with the acquisition of personhood: When in the history of human evolution is personhood acquired?

Different from these biological points is the question of the legality of the efforts at the state level to declare personhood with fertilization. The Supreme Court has held that personhood is acquired with viability; i.e., about twenty-four to twenty-eight weeks (*Roe v. Wade*). Thus, if a state effort should succeed, a lengthy court will surely be required to resolve the conflict.

As said previously, it is necessary from a practical point of view to select one of the events previously described as THE event that indicates personhood. In the view of this observer, the Supreme Court probably got it right. Viability, the ability to survive without being attached to the mother is surely THE major biological milestone indicating personhood. All interested should read the Preamble to the Supreme Court decision where the history of attempts of mankind to select the spot is reviewed.

Personhood, therefore, remains a subject of much discussion. The matter is very much alive. The problem can be solved only by much public discussion and to determine whether the present legal position of the United States as decreed by *Roe v. Wade* is, as I believe, the best possible solution, or perhaps there is another. It can be decided only by much public discussion.

# *Eight*

## *The Worldwide Surveillance of In Vitro Fertilization*

*Work with the Ethics Committee of the American Fertility Society* in attempting to devise guidelines for use in the United States naturally led to the question of what was being done in other countries. Indeed, by the late '80s almost all countries where there was a major IVF effort had produced guidelines or, in some cases, legislation specifically directed at the IVF treatment of reproductive failure. It seemed important, therefore, to tabulate what other countries thought with a view to understanding what other countries were surveying, and more particularly to try to understand exactly what it was that society, in general, wished to monitor.

This proposition was discussed with my long-standing friend, the late Dr. Jean Cohen of Paris, France. Jean Cohen, at that time, happened to be president of the International Federation of Fertility Societies (IFFS), but, more than that, he was one of the real pioneers in IVF. Jean thought this was a good idea. He furthermore suggested that it might be done under the aegis of the IFFS, giving it a true international flavor under an important imprimatur. He also undertook approaching several possible funding sources for this, and succeeded in getting the attention of the Organon Company, particularly Dr. Henk J. Out. The Organon Company agreed to underwrite the development and publication costs of such a project.

Accordingly, a questionnaire was developed covering many of the items that had been considered in the ethics report of the American Fertility Society and this questionnaire was distributed internationally in early 1998 with the request that the respondents document the situation as of December 31, 1997. The questionnaire was distributed to thirty-eight countries considered to be the most active in the IVF procedure.

The general purpose of the project was stated in the publication, which resulted from the distribution of the questionnaires, that publication appearing as a supplement to *Fertility and Sterility* in May 1999. It was entitled, "IFFS Surveillance 98." The general purpose was as follows:

> Internationally, there are several examples of medical/ scientific naiveté expressed in legislation aimed at the surveillance of assisted reproductive technology.
>
> One example will illustrate the point. Some countries have enacted legislation that allows cryopreservation of embryos, (the word "embryo" is used in the Surveillance report to indicate any state of development after fertilization), but does not permit the retention of the cryopreserved material for more than one year. This legislation in effect prevents a couple who has achieved a term pregnancy from using the cryopreserved material, as very few couples who achieved such a pregnancy will wish to initiate a subsequent pregnancy within a year of the initiation of the

successful pregnancy.

Such contradictive legislative actions are likely due to pressure from special interest groups, and from the absence of an authoritative international document setting forth what the medical/scientific community regards as medically and scientifically feasible and desirable.

The purpose of an international conference under the aegis of the International Federation of Fertility Societies was to provide such a document. In order to achieve this goal, medical/scientific representatives from sovereign nations were asked to consider the medical/scientific feasibility and desirability of various assisted reproductive technology procedures without regard to any previous or existing ethical, cultural, religious, or legal pronouncements about the particular procedure under consideration.

Any resulting document from the conference would therefore hopefully be the result of natural reason with the influence of medical/scientific experience openly acknowledged. The exclusion of contemporary ethical, cultural, religious, and legal attitudes does not mean that what is medically/scientifically possible is necessarily desirable.

The goal was to give the medical/scientific community an opportunity to express its unfettered experience, which has traditionally held that the goal of the healer is to enhance the good of the individual or individuals, all things considered.

The rationale of carrying it out was stated in the Preface, as follows:

The development of in vitro fertilization (IVF) and its
subsequent variations and extensions, all now included
under the umbrella of assisted reproductive technology (ART), seems to have generated more interest and
concern among religious leaders, bioethicists, and the
general public than any other medical procedure ever
devised. This widespread interest and concern attract-
ed the attention of, or was called to the attention of,
the political process, not only by ethicists and moral
theologians, but by consumer groups, some members
of which expressed dissatisfaction with one or another
aspect of their treatment or lack of access thereto.

As a result of these events, a very large number
of committees and commissions, some governmental,
some not, have examined the ethical, legal, religious,
medical, and public policy aspects of ART, eventuat-
ing in the establishments of guidelines and/or government regulations in many, but not all, sovereign states
practicing ART. For the purpose of this discussion, the
word "guidelines" will be used to designate sets of rules
to be followed voluntarily and the word "regulations"
will be used to designate sets of rules adopted by legislative action with assigned penalties for violations.

Such guidelines/regulations have taken a variety
of forms and have often expressed not only a particular
medical perspective but also sometimes reflected the
social and religious mores of the particular sovereign
state. Some of the guidelines/regulations have been
formulated to accommodate special interest groups.

Furthermore, surveillance of compliance with
guidelines/regulations has taken a variety of forms
from none at all to the issuance of a license by a gov-

ernmental licensing body, after fulfilling designated requirements, and often including periodic follow-up inspections.

The specific purposes of this project are:

1 Tabulation of the practice of sovereign nations or political subdivisions thereof with respect to the adoption of guidelines/regulations.
2 Tabulation of the methods of surveillance, if any, of such guidelines/regulations.
3 Tabulation of the similarities and differences of the guidelines/regulations themselves concerning the various procedures under the umbrella of ART and especially to identify within the guidelines/ regulations any that may be medically naïve or contradictory, or not supportive of the best interest of the patients, their families, and society in general.
4 Attempting to develop a document under the aegis of the International Federation of Fertility Societies (IFFS) insofar as such a document is possible concerning the items referred to in the three items above. The purpose of such a document under the aegis of an internationally respected scientific body, i.e., IFFS, is to serve as a reference source for committees or commissions, or legislative bodies, which are charged with formulating or revising guidelines/regulations for any entity expected to practice any aspect of ART or to exercise surveillance.

The material was categorized more or less as the material was for the American Fertility Society, though it had to be modified because of its international nature, and in the end, it was categorized in twelve chapters as follows:

1 Legislation and guidelines (surveillance): Howard W. Jones, Jr., Eastern Virginia Medical School, The Howard and Georgeanna Jones Institute for Reproductive Medicine, 601 Colley Avenue, Norfolk, Virginia.

2 Marital status in ART: Joseph G. Schenker, Hadassah Eink Karem Hospital, Jerusalem, Israel.

3 ART—The number to transfer: Howard W. Jones, Jr.

4 Cryopreservation: Ester Polak de Fried, CER Medical Institute, Department of Reproductive Medicine, Humboldt 2263, (1425) Buenos Aires, Argentina.

5 Donation of gametes and embryos: Francoise Shenfield, University College Hospital, Huntley Street, London, UK.

6 Micromanipulation: Gamal I. Serour, The Egyptian IVF–IT Center, Made, Cairo, Egypt.

7 Welfare of the child: Francoise Shenfield.

8 Embryo reduction: Joseph G. Schenker.

9 Preimplantation genetic diagnosis: Joseph G. Schenker.

10 IVF surrogacy: Joseph G. Schenker.

11 Embryo research: Douglas Saunders, Department of Obstetrics and Gynecology, University of Sydney, Wallace Freeborn Professorial Block, Royal North Shore Hospital, Sydney, Australia.

12 Cloning: Joseph G. Schenker.

After codification, each of the six individuals was asked to prepare a proposed summary statement concerning their particular subheading. These proposed summary statements were presented for consideration, discussion, modification, and adoption at a special meeting held in San Francisco, California, USA, October 3, 1998, immediately before the IFFS/ASRM meeting.

It was hoped that the documentation of the great variation in what was being surveyed in the various countries might lead to a consensus if these variations were discussed in an international forum. Therefore, the 1998 data were presented to the national delegates who had participated in the 1998 survey at the International Federation of Fertility Societies meeting in San Francisco, California in October 1998 in the hope that at least some of these discrepancies brought out by the survey could be resolved. However, this effort had limited success, as the delegates were concerned that they were not empowered to authorize a deviation from the situation as revealed by the survey. Thus, consensus could not be obtained and, indeed, the San Francisco concurrence effort in subsequent publications of surveillance data has not been repeated, as it seemed unlikely that a consensus could be gathered for the reason mentioned.

Surveillance by guidelines and legislation has continued to evolve and the questionnaire survey sponsored by the Organon Company under the aegis of the IFFS was repeated and published in 2001, 2004, 2007, and 2010. The status of the situation is covered by the preface to the 2007 publication, as follows:

> An e-mail survey was developed and one or more individuals from the principal sovereign nations were

invited to respond. Answers were obtained from 57 countries, but not all questions were answered in all responses. This explains why in some of the tables that follow some information is not given. The number of centers is an estimate and should not be taken as fact. The coordinators (Natalia van Houten and Keith Gordon) prepared the tables under the various sub-headings matched to the questionnaire. The analysis of the survey was prepared by the editors: Jean Cohen, M.D.; Howard Jones, Jr., M.D.; Ian Cooke, M.D.; and Roger Kempers, M.D.

This report, "IFFS Surveillance 07" summarizes the various laws, regulations, and/or guidelines established by fifty-seven nations to regulate and oversee the medical practice of ART.

The most striking finding is the great diversity in these laws and guidelines. The following two questions immediately arise:

1 Why does society wish to oversee ART as op-posed to other specific medical procedures?
2 What exactly does society wish to oversee?

An answer to both questions may arise princi-pally from a single source. Historically, there was great objection to the work of the pioneers in IVF. This pro-test was from a variety of organizations, all under the umbrella of the religious right. Although objections took various forms, the essence of the complaints was that IVF resulted in the destruction of some fertilized eggs, which were considered by the objectors to have the moral status of a human already in being, in other words, of a human being.

It must also be said and emphasized that many religious organizations of various persuasions, as well as a large segment of the population, take the position that the developing human conceptus does not deserve protection by society during early development, which is the situation in the clinical application of IVF.

The divergent views concerning the moral status of the developing embryo are likely the chief cause of the divergent rules and guidelines, because pressure is exerted by adversary groups and individuals on those responsible for enacting such laws or guidelines. The very fact that it has been necessary to adopt laws or guidelines probably is itself an expression of the tension arising from the various points of view about moral status.

If this analysis is correct, it appears that a consensus on the necessity for and the method of surveillance of ART is unlikely in the foreseeable future. Even physicians and scientists can reflect the societal influences and thought that surround them.

Meanwhile, one hopes that "IFFS Surveillance 07" will prove to be a source of information about these matters and will stimulate more discussion of why and what society is trying to achieve by its monitoring of ART.

Between the 2007 and 2010 edition of the IFFS international survey, the sponsorship shifted to Schering–Plough Pharmaceutical Company. Furthermore, the process became entirely electronic and the results made available on the website of the International Federation of Fertility Societies. Ian Cooke of Sheffield, UK, assumed the leadership; Peter Brinsden, emeritus director of the Bourn Hall Clinic outside of Cambridge, England, and Douglas Saunders, emeritus professor at the University of Sydney in Australia and an IVF pioneer, joined the editorship.

The 2010 report was expanded to cover one hundred and seven nations. The legislative situation was summarized in the report as follows (Table 8, "IFFS 2010"):

> Among the 103 nations with reliable information on this point, 42 operated with legislative oversight, 26 with voluntary guidelines, and 35 operated with neither. In some instances, this subdivision is somewhat arbitrary. For instance, the United States can clearly be labeled as a guideline country and yet if a program were to use donor eggs, donor sperm, or donor embryos, these would fall under regulations promulgated by the Federal Drug Administration. In Australia, the situation is somewhat ambiguous. All clinics are required by law to be accredited. The penalty for operating a non-accredited clinic is up to 10 years in jail. However, there are no specific penalties for breaching the Australian Code of Practice other than withdrawal of accreditation if compliance actions are not satisfactorily attended to.
>
> In the entities where clinical ART functions under legislation, the legislation usually includes regulation governing the operation of the embryological laboratory. However, there are some exceptions, for instance, Armenia, Brazil, Iceland, Indonesia, Kosovo, Russia, Singapore, Spain, Sweden, and Vietnam. In guideline countries, the guidelines usually include guidelines for

embryological laboratories but there are exceptions. For instance, Argentina, Belarus, Iceland, Ivory Coast, Poland, and Ukraine have no embryological laboratory guidelines. Curiously enough, it seems that the countries that do not have embryological laboratory guidelines do not have separate laws governing the operation of the embryological laboratory. However, among countries that operate without legislation and without guidelines, there are some countries which have laws governing embryological practice. Such is the case with Bosnia, Colombia, the Democratic Republic of the Congo, the Dominican Republic, Nigeria, Romania, Slovenia, and Sudan.

About two-thirds of the countries operating under legislation have licensing bodies. The United Kingdom is a prototype for that arrangement. The Human Fertilisation and Embryological Authority (HFEA) requires that all programs before the issue of a license demonstrate that they can comply with a Code of Practice, which is constantly updated by HFEA and which covers all details of the clinical and embryological practice associated with assisted reproductive technology.

Furthermore, if research is to be conducted by a particular programme, a special license is also required from the HFEA. HFEA issues an annual report of end results without identification of individual clinics. Some programmes of IVF may have a quasi-licensing aspect. For example, in the United States the Society for Assisted Reproductive Technology (SART), a subsidiary of the American Society for Reproductive Medicine (ASRM), issues a certificate to programs which adhere to the most recently published ASRM minimal standards for IVF and ART, maintain a high level of ethical and moral standards and submit annual data to the SART registry as mandated by the Fertility Clinic Success Rate and Certification Act (Wyden legislation). It is possible however for programmes to operate without being certified by SART and approximately 10% of clinics in the United States so operate. If one is a member in good standing of SART and there is some violation of the above-mentioned regulations, SART does have the opportunity to withdraw its certification. However, this really has little impact.

Individuals in programmes which are in violation of the standards promulgated from time to time by ASRM, either by the Ethics Committee or the Practice Committee, can be expelled from ASRM. Indeed, that was the situation with the doctor who was responsible for the octuplets in California in 2009. Patients would need to be aware of these actions for there to be any effect. It is also worth mentioning that a considerable body of civil law has arisen in spite of legislation and rules and regulations. The United States might be again cited as an example. Since IVF has been widely practiced clinically, there have been tried in the civil and appellate courts well over 1,000 cases involving various aspects of the practice of assisted reproductive technology. These include such things as the custody of a frozen embryo in divorce cases, the parental claims by surrogates, the question of whether IVF is covered in insurance contracts, and in addition, of course, liability claims when some error has been made, as for example, the loss of embryos or the transfer of nonparental embryos.

It is to be noted that in legislative countries in which severe penalties are imposed for violation of the code, all penalties are applied to the practitioners and to the clinic and there appears to be no country with legislation which is directed toward the patient for being involved in a procedure that is in violation of the legislation. It is difficult to document to what degree legislation and guidelines are followed in detail. There is abundant evidence however to suggest that violations of some aspects may be widespread. The United States can again be used as an example where the incidence of multiple pregnancies cannot be accounted for except by violation of the guidelines as to the number to be transferred as reported in the annual SART report.

Not covered by the survey, but of interest, is the fact that there is at least one country, namely Costa Rica, in which IVF is prohibited. This is the result of an action by the constitutional court of that country in which it is stated that personhood begins with fertilization and it has therefore been interpreted to indicate that since there may be some destruction of early embryos which are involved in IVF, IVF is not practiced at all in that nation.

In the 2007 IFFS Surveillance, 58 countries were surveyed. In the current 2010 Surveillance, 107 countries have been surveyed. This great increase in the number of countries surveyed has resulted in a substantial shift in the percentage of countries covered by legislation as opposed to guidelines or neither one. In the 2007 Surveillance, some 50% of countries were covered by legislation, whereas in the 2010

Surveillance, this had dropped to 42%. On the other hand, in 2007 only 19% of the countries had neither legislation nor guidelines, but that figure is now 35% in the 2010 report. These changes are probably not as significant as they seem because many of the recently added countries are from the developing world where there has been insufficient time for guidelines or legislation to be adopted. One can speculate that in further reports the number of legislative countries or guideline countries will increase at the expense of the countries operating with neither.

There is some evidence that in legislation in some countries, the legislation has been more influenced by the social background of the legislative body of the country than by the goal of good medical practice. These are exceptional countries and Italy is the prime example. On the other hand, in most countries where there is legislation, there can be little doubt that the guiding principle has been an effort to practice good medicine. Legislation, which is regarded as restrictive by the patient population, has led to a certain amount of reproductive tourism to overcome the restrictive aspects of the legislation.

| Country | Statutes | Guidelines | None | Licensing body | Statutes incl. embryo lab practice | Guidelines incl. embryo lab practice | Neither incl. embryo lab practice |
|---|---|---|---|---|---|---|---|
| Abu Dhabi | + | – | – | + | + | | |
| Albania | + | – | – | + | – | | |
| Algeria | + | – | – | – | + | | |
| Argentina | – | – | + | | | | – |
| Armenia | + | – | – | + | – | | |
| Australia | – | + | – | + | | | + |
| Austria | + | – | – | + | + | | – |
| Bangladesh | – | – | + | | | | |
| Belarus | – | + | – | | | | – |
| Belgium | + | – | – | + | + | | |
| Bosnia | – | – | + | | | | + |
| Brazil | + | – | – | + | – | | |
| Bulgaria | + | – | – | | + | | |
| Burkina Faso | – | – | + | | | | |
| Cameroon | – | + | – | | | + | |
| Canada | + | – | – | + | + | | |
| Chile | – | + | – | | | + | |
| China | – | + | – | | | + | |
| Colombia | – | – | + | – | | | + |
| Congo | – | – | + | | | | – |
| Croatia | + | – | – | + | + | | |
| Cuba | – | + | – | | | + | |
| Cyprus | – | + | – | | | + | |
| Czech Rep | + | – | – | + | + | | |
| Dem Rep Congo | – | – | + | | | | + |
| Denmark | + | – | – | + | + | | |
| Dominican Rep | – | – | + | | | | + |
| Ecuador | – | – | + | | | | |
| Egypt | – | + | – | | | + | |
| El Salvador | – | – | + | | | | – |
| Estonia | + | – | – | + | + | | – |
| Ethiopia | – | – | + | | | | |
| Finland | + | – | – | + | + | | |
| France | + | – | – | + | + | | |

National Regulation of Art.

| Country | Statutes | Guidelines | None | Licensing body | Statutes incl. embryo lab practice | Guidelines incl. embryo lab practice | Neither incl. embryo lab practice |
|---|---|---|---|---|---|---|---|
| Germany | + | − | − | + | + | | |
| Ghana | − | + | − | | | + | |
| Greece | + | − | − | + | + | | |
| Hong Kong | + | − | − | + | + | | |
| Hungary | + | − | − | + | + | | |
| Iceland | + | − | − | − | − | | |
| India | − | + | − | | | + | |
| Indonesia | + | ... | ... | + | ... | | |
| Iran | + | − | − | + | + | | |
| Ireland | − | + | − | | | − | |
| Israel | + | − | − | + | + | | |
| Italy | + | − | − | + | + | | |
| Ivory Coast | − | + | − | | | − | |
| Jamaica | − | − | + | | | | − |
| Japan | − | + | − | | | + | |
| Jordan | − | − | + | | | | − |
| Korea | + | − | − | + | + | | |
| Kosovo | + | − | − | + | − | | |
| Kuwait | − | + | − | | | + | |
| Latvia | − | − | + | | | | − |
| Lebanon | − | − | − | | | | − |
| Libya | − | + | − | + | | + | |
| Lithuania | − | − | + | | | | − |
| Malaysia | − | − | + | | | | − |
| Mali | − | − | + | | | | |
| Mexico | − | + | − | | | + | |
| Montenegro | + | − | − | + | + | | |
| Morocco | − | − | + | | | | − |
| Namibia | − | − | + | | | | − |
| Nepal | − | − | + | | | | − |
| Netherlands | + | − | − | + | + | | |
| New Zealand | + | − | − | + | + | | |
| Nigeria | − | − | + | | | | + |
| Norway | + | − | − | + | + | | |
| Pakistan | − | − | + | | | | − |
| Panama | − | − | + | | | | − |

National Regulation of Art.

| Country | Statutes | Guidelines | None | Licensing body | Statutes incl. embryo lab practice | Guidelines incl. embryo lab practice | Neither incl. embryo lab practice |
|---|---|---|---|---|---|---|---|
| Paraguay | − | − | + | | | | − |
| Peru | − | − | + | | | | − |
| Philippines | − | + | − | | | | |
| Poland | − | + | − | | | | − |
| Portugal | + | − | − | + | + | | |
| Romania | − | − | + | | | | + |
| Russia | + | − | − | + | + | | |
| Saudi Arabia | − | + | − | | | | |
| Senegal | − | − | + | | | | − |
| Serbia | − | + | − | | | + | |
| Singapore | + | − | − | + | + | | |
| Slovakia | + | − | − | | − | | |
| Slovenia | − | − | + | | | | + |
| South Africa | + | − | − | | + | | |
| Spain | + | − | − | + | + | | |
| Sri Lanka | − | + | − | | | | |
| Sudan | − | − | + | | | | + |
| Swaziland | − | − | = | | | | − |
| Sweden | + | − | − | | − | | |
| Switzerland | + | − | − | + | + | | |
| Taiwan | + | − | − | + | + | + | |
| Thailand | − | + | − | | | | |
| Togo | − | − | + | | | | − |
| Trinidad/Tobago | − | − | + | | | | − |
| Tunisia | + | − | − | + | + | | |
| Turkey | + | − | − | + | + | | |
| Uganda | − | − | + | | | | − |
| UK | + | − | − | + | + | | |
| Ukraine | − | + | − | | | − | |
| Uruguay | − | − | + | | | | − |
| USA | − | + | − | | | + | |
| Venezuela | − | + | − | | | + | |
| Vietnam | + | − | − | + | − | | |
| Zimbabwe | − | − | + | | | | − |

National Regulation of Art.

Because of the cultural differences in the various counties, it seems unlikely that in the foreseeable future a consensus can be reached. This is regrettable, as it would be hoped that the medical scientific community using reason could devise a set of guidelines that would be applicable to all societies, but the world is not yet at that point.

# *Nine*

## *Assisted Reproductive Technology and the Law*

### A Suit for Libel

*As noted in a previous section, the initiation of the IVF program* stimulated opposition from a segment of the population. This took various forms, one of which was letters to the editor, and editorials in the local newspaper, *The Virginian Pilot*.

During the first week of 1982, an editorial appeared in that paper celebrating the opening of a Hardy House, which offers special services to mentally handicapped children, especially children whose handicap is congenital in origin. A portion of the editorial stated:

> Mere blocks away from the Hardy House was born this week the nation's first test tube baby. No such baby will ever become candidates for Hardy House because no "defective" fetus will ever be permitted to survive the mother's womb.

A few weeks later a distinguished local attorney, Mr. Robert Nusbaum, came to my office. I knew him only slightly, but I did know that he was a long-time and good friend of Mason Andrews. Mr. Nusbaum said that he had admired the work of the in vitro group and he was distressed by all of the opposition that it had created; he further went on to say that he had turned over in his mind possible avenues to prevent such opposition. He said he had come to the conclusion that only some major development would alter the attitude of the paper and he said it may be that that opportunity had presented itself in the Hardy House editorial. He said that this editorial had all the earmarks of libel and that we should consider suing the newspaper for libel. If the suit were to be successful that would surely put an end to a good bit of the opposition. He pointed out the earmarks of libel with one of the points being that the editorial writer had to know that he was stating a situation that really did not exist. Mr. Nusbaum pointed out that he had good information that the editorial writer, Terry Eastland, had been warned that Norfolk patients were not required to sign an agreement to terminate a defective baby such as indicated in the editorial and as was thought to be the case with Edwards and Steptoe in England.

At first the notion to sue seemed like a monstrous suggestion. We were heavily involved in trying to unravel the scientific difficulties that we ran into and without knowing any of the details, it seemed that this would require a great deal of time. However, Mr. Nusbaum was rather confident that he would be successful.

The editorial had referred to "those doctors at EVMS." There were five possibilities: Mason Andrews, Anibal Acosta, Jairo Garcia, Georgeanna Jones, and myself (Howard Jones). Mr. Nusbaum said that it wasn't necessary for all five to sue the newspaper but that it would be practical for one to sue the newspaper and if later on things went well, the others could join the suit. He recommended that that person be the one least likely to be combative, and it was generally agreed that that one person was Georgeanna. Furthermore, it was pointed out that in the initiation of the suit it was not necessary to specify a particular amount of money that we were suing for because under the laws of libel the amount of the award had to be commensurate with the resources of the defendant. He said that if the suit progressed well enough at some point the defendant would have to disclose their assets and at that point a suitable amount could be determined.

Therefore, with this arrangement Georgeanna entered suit early in 1982 and during the summer of 1982 much time was consumed by all five members of the team in doing things that we didn't know anything about, such as discovery, depositions, and the like. It was exceedingly time-consuming. During the deposition, it was clearly brought out that there wasn't the slightest basis to the notion that patients had to sign a document to undergo an elective termination of pregnancy in the event an abnormality was found.

In January 1983, when Landmark Communications, the parent of *The Virginian Pilot,* became aware that there might possibly be a lawsuit, they published what they defined as a clarification in which they said, "Some doctors involved in the Norfolk program have inferred that the writer intended to describe their personal attitudes toward abortion. No such consideration was intended. *The Virginian Pilot* regrets any inference to the contrary and apologizes to any participant in the clinic who perceives the words as a characterization of his or her professional attitudes, beliefs, or conduct."

This "clarification" was insufficient to avoid the pursuit for libel according to Mr. Nusbaum's judgment. During the deposition, it became clear that there was an attempt on the part of the attorney for Landmark Communication to indicate that the real reason for the lawsuit was not the question of abortion. He stated, "I think that these plaintiffs decided that they were going to look for a lawsuit to discipline the newspaper. They filed the suit not because they were damaged but they wanted to control the newspaper coverage." The implication of this attitude was that the suit amounted to an attempt to infringe upon the paper's right to free expression.

In December of 1982, the depositions were completed. Mr. Nusbaum was quite satisfied with the way they went and suggested that the other four doctors join the suit and this, indeed, was done.

It then came time for Landmark Communications to reveal their assets so that the amount of money requested in the suit would be sufficient to damage the assets of the defendant. Before this part of the proceedings took place, two very prominent Norfolk citizens, Mr. Henry Clay Hofheimer and Dr. Robert Payne, came to see the five doctors. They said that this lawsuit was separating the community, that the community was choosing up sides and they thought that this was contrary to the best interest of all concerned and they wanted to know whether they could act as intermediaries to try to work out a settlement between Landmark Communications and the five doctors.

The five doctors differed in their reactions to this suggestion, but after due consideration, it was decided that in the best interest of the community, we should allow Mr. Hofheimer and Dr. Payne to see what they could work out. Accordingly, a meeting was arranged between Mr. Frank Batten, the owner of Landmark Communications, and Georgeanna in Mr. Hofheimer's office. Georgeanna was the only one to meet, as she was the original plaintiff. At the meeting, Georgeanna started off by apologizing to Mr. Batten for the problem that she had caused. She said that if this had happened in Baltimore she happened to know the people who owned the *Baltimore Sun* and she would have gone to them to try to straighten this out; she also apologized that she didn't first come to Mr. Batten to explain the problem. In turn, Mr. Batten apologized to Georgeanna and said the paper was sorry that it had done what it had done and he was prepared to arrange for a settlement.

Accordingly, a settlement was made and the suit settled. By the terms of the settlement, it was agreed that the amount of money that changed hands would not be disclosed. However, the five doctors had agreed ahead of time that in the event that funds were received each of them would donate those funds to the Eastern Virginia Medical School Foundation for research in the IVF program. Accordingly, this was done. Thus, the suit for libel provided research funds for four or five years and I have often said that this money was much easier to acquire than trying to get money from a research grant submitted to the National Institutes of Health.

**Testifying Before Congress**

On August 8–9, 1984, there was a hearing before the Subcommittee on Investigations and Oversights of the Committee on Science and Technology of the House of Representatives. This hearing took place in Washington, D.C., and Dr. Gary Hodgen and I were invited to testify before the committee at its first session on August 8. The chairman of that committee was none other than Mr. Al Gore, at that time a representative from the state of Tennessee. In his opening statement, he pointed out that approximately six hundred children had been born worldwide as the result of in vitro fertilization and that there were two or possibly three of these children born of frozen embryos.

He went on to point out that the potential use of some of these techniques challenge our traditional notion about parenting, adoption, inheritance, and motherhood, and they are forcing a reevaluation of both our legal and ethical understandings. He pointed out that very recently the British government had released the Warnock Report covering these areas and that in Australia the Waller Commission was studying the ethical and legal implications of this type of birth. He went on further to say that unfortunately here in the United States we have yet to grapple with these issues in spite of the fact that the American Fertility Society had adopted certain criteria. He further said that in the hearings he hoped to begin a responsible dialogue on these sensitive issues and look to how a consensus on these issues might be developed.

He then called on Dr. Clifford Grobstein, professor of biological sciences and public policy at the University of California, San Diego. Professor Grobstein was to be an important part of the Ethics Committee of the American Fertility Society. Grobstein presented the view that it would be very desirable to establish a suitable deliberating mechanism for the whole range of new reproductive options, listing particularly eight points:

1  To define the status of the human embryo so as to protect its unique value in human society
2  To define and protect parental rights with respect to the new options
3  To alleviate infertility
4  To reduce genetic disease and birth defects, as feasible
5  To maximize freedom of research while protecting essential human rights

6  To reduce legal conflict and confusion
7  To minimize regulatory actions that may under-
   mine professional initiative and responsibilities
8  To maximize public understanding and
   participation

I was the next witness called. I offered a prepared statement, which was incorporated in the records. I pointed out that
in vitro fertilization had been accepted as a standard method of
therapy by the American Fertility Society and that operational
and ethical guidelines had been adopted by the Fertility Society
and the American College of Obstetricians and Gynecologists.
I then discussed the details of IVF, the possibility of using donor sperm and donor eggs, and the possibility of cryopreservation. About an hour into my testimony, I noticed that Barbara
Brooks, carrying her four-month-old IVF son, Daniel; Pamela
Cakora; Patricia Grimaldi; and some other Norfolk IVF mothers, had entered the room. I therefore asked Representative
Gore if I could ask some of the Washington mothers of in vitro
fertilization to stand. He granted permission to do so and they
did. Mr. Gore asked them to remain standing for a moment
and said that it was wonderful to see them. He congratulated
everybody.

This was really a turning point in the hearing. Mr. Gore
had been, I thought, somewhat critical of the lack of supervision , but after Barbara Brooks appeared with the IVF mothers,
his attitude changed completely. The fact is that he came down
off the bench, went over to the mothers, shook each of their
hands, and held the baby as a sign of his interest and respect.

Gary Hodgen then testified about scientific aspects and
after that, Mr. Gore turned to me again and said, "Dr. Jones, in
my opinion, most Americans realize very clearly what a blessing

it is for all these mothers. Nevertheless, questions do remain in spite of the guidelines put out by the American Fertility Society and the American College." He asked, "In your view, do they suffice to deal with the bioethical conditions that confront your practice?"

I replied that I thought they did.

He then asked, "What is the overseeing body?" and expressed interest that there was no oversight.

I pointed out that there was oversight by the general public.

He asked what the penalties were for violation.

I pointed out it was the penalty of the criticisms of one's colleagues.

He did not seem to think that this was adequate supervision and said, "Often it's the case that in these new areas there is a heightened sensitivity during the early stages and then after the practice is continued for a generation there is a kind of lapse. He was concerned that there would be an ultimate lack of sensitivity to bioethical questions. He then asked about genetic manipulation. I pointed out that this was something far in the future, but he said maybe not so far. It was on this note that the hearing adjourned for the morning.

Many other individuals spoke on the same topics and other topics undergoing evaluation, such as uterine flushing to obtain fertilized eggs to give to infertile recipients. It is extremely interesting and significant that after these hearings, and in spite of Mr. Gore's concern about the ethical matter that he expressed and in spite of the fact of the Warnock Commission in the UK and the Waller Commission in Australia, the Congress of the United States did not attempt to adopt any kind of regulatory mechanism.

It was only several years later after hearings before the

Wyden Committee that a reporting mechanism was developed and not until the twenty-first century that the FDA exerted certain regulatory mechanisms for donor material.

## The Legal Status of the Fertilized Egg

The in vitro fertilization program at Norfolk was among the first to cryopreserve excess fertilized eggs and, indeed, reported to the CDC in conforming to the Wyden law the first term pregnancy in the United States from a cryopreserved fertilized egg.

In 1988, we had a request by a patient who lived in California to allow her to take her remaining cryopreserved fertilized egg to California where there was now a program that could implant the cryopreserved material into her uterus. She had come to Norfolk and had an unsuccessful IVF attempt with fresh eggs.

In 1988, shipment of human cryopreserved eggs or fertilized eggs was not practiced and had never been done. The patient proposed that she come to Norfolk and pick up the egg and take it with her back to California.

The Norfolk program had several concerns:

1  It could not quite understand the motive of the patient because it would certainly not save her any money in that she had to make the journey to Norfolk to pick up the egg to take it back to California for implantation.
2  The Norfolk program had no knowledge of the capability of the California program to handle the cryopreserved material. The question arose as to what responsibility the Norfolk program had to ascertain this.

3   Most importantly, the Norfolk program was
    concerned about liability, that is to say in the
    event something happened—whatever it could be:
    the egg did not survive the journey, the egg was
    lost, and so on—what legal responsibility did the
    Norfolk program have in the event any of these
    things should happen.

4   Finally, the thought did occur that we were unsure
    that the patient really would have the egg im-
    planted in herself. It would be entirely possible to
    give the egg to a third party, or even to sell it.

Because of these concerns, the Norfolk program declined
the patient's request and for a few months there had been no
further discussion. Completely out of the blue and without
further discussion, the Norfolk program found that it had been
sued in the Federal Circuit Court over possession of the cryopreserved fertilized egg (*York v. Jones*, 1989).

The trial judge did indeed award the fertilized egg to the
patient, but he granted the Norfolk program complete im-
munity from any untoward event that might occur. A most
interesting aspect of the case was the civil status assigned to the
cryopreserved fertilized egg by the judge. He referred to these
eggs as *chattel*, i.e., "things."

This contrasted the civil status assigned to cryopreserved
fertilized eggs in the *Davis v. Davis* case: in 1990 the trial judge
applied the rules of custody to the eggs, thus, implying personhood. However, in the *Davis v. Davis* situation, the Appellate
Court in 1993 reversed the trial judge and assigned a status
consistent with that described in the Ethics Committee Report
of the American Fertility Society in 1986; that is, he said the
cryopreserved fertilized eggs were not persons but deserved

respect in light of their human origin.

There have been relatively few further cases that have directly addressed the question of the civil and moral status of the cryopreserved or non-cryopreserved fertilized eggs in the status between fertilization in vitro and transfer to the uterus.

## Legal Conceptions

IVF and ART, which is defined as the technology in which gametes from both partners are processed in a laboratory, as might be expected from any new clinical technology, gave rise to situations that required decision by a court of law.

Susan Crockin, a young lawyer from Massachusetts, became involved in these legal matters. She brought these cases to the attention of the reproductive community by a regular page in the periodical *Fertility News*, the news bulletin of the American Fertility Society. By 2010, the cases narrated in abstract were well over a thousand and it seemed appropriate to collect and publish these with both legal and medical comments. Susan Crockin asked me to collaborate in the book, which was titled *Legal Conceptions*, and the book was published in 2010 by The Johns Hopkins University Press.

*Legal Conceptions.*

The background, purpose, origin, and goal of this publication are well set forth by the preface of *Legal Conceptions*:

> By 1990 it had become clear to the courts that "the in vitro fertilization genie is out of the bottle and you can't put it back." The first divorce dispute over frozen embryos, *Davis v. Davis*, had erupted and captured the nation's attention as an intriguing "brave new world" fight over "preembryos" and all the competing views and values attendant to them. As *Nightline* and Ted Koppel aired the dispute night after night, the legal issues in this case were highlighted, as other fertility-related disputes were percolating up through the courts.
>
> It seemed to this lawyer that the time had come to gather and share legal information and insights into how the courts were both viewing and responding to the issues surrounding these new families and the medical professionals whose talents and energies had made them possible. The idea for "Legally Speaking" was born. In 1990, this author proposed, wrote, and submitted a pilot column to the American Fertility Society (now the American Society for Reproductive Medicine) entitled, "Legally Speaking: A Column Highlighting Recent Court Decisions Affecting the Assisted Reproductive Technologies (ART) and the Families They Create." It was accepted by the board of AFS on an experimental basis, to be published in *Fertility News*, which was issued four or five times a year, with a distribution to all members of the Society. That experiment has now spanned twenty years, almost a hundred columns, with reports on close to a thousand legal cases, statutes, and developments.

In December 1990, "Legally Speaking"™ debuted in *Fertility News*. It reported on six novel assisted reproductive technology–related court cases. Remarkably, each of those cases addressed issues that still vex courts today. In addition to the Davis dispute over frozen embryos, the column reported on the first parental claim by a gestational carrier (*Johnson v. Calvert*); a successful challenge to insurance coverage for infertility treatment (without a statutory mandate); a class action lawsuit by doctors asserting that Illinois's statute banning fetal experimentation was having a chilling effect on their research; a known sperm donor's assertion of paternity rights over a child he helped a lesbian couple to conceive; and a prisoner claiming an unconstitutional denial of access to artificial insemination services.

Unique among analyses of legal developments, "Legally Speaking" has reported in real time and in plain English on hundreds of court cases and legal developments as novel lawsuits were filed, appealed, settled, or decided and as legislation moved through the process from bills and revisions to laws or vetoes. By reporting on developing cases and legislation instead of merely the final decision or legal bottom line, "Legally Speaking" has been able to illustrate, and thereby aid professionals in the field to understand, the changing legal landscape within which their actions and decisions are questioned and ultimately judged. To help contextualize the developing law and policy in the United States, selected international developments were also reported, as were selected non-ART cases that raised issues such as professional liability with respect to patients in other contexts, genetic testing claims, stem cell research, wrongful life and birth claims, and discrimination in health care, to name but a few.

The litigation covered in *Legal Conceptions* is quite varied and includes cases from clinical and laboratory errors to problems of paternity, maternity, custody, financial responsibility, ownership, and other aspects of assisted reproductive technology, particularly concerning donor gametes and surrogacy.

As with most innovative technologies, the law follows after the establishment of the technologies. This is the usual nature of such things; thus, the law will continue to evolve as the technology of reproduction evolves.

# Ten

## The Future of IVF

*Prior to 1980, if an infertile couple went to an expert in the* field, there would be approximately a 50 percent probability that the problem could be solved, even using donor sperm for male infertility. However, some thirty years after the beginning of IVF, the probability of a couple achieving a normal baby is essentially 100 percent with two important provisos— first, that the couple is prepared to deal with the problem until the desired result is obtained, and, second, that they are prepared, if necessary, as it sometimes is, to use donor gametes when reproductive aging or other causes result in defects in the sperm or eggs. In addition, it may be necessary sometimes to borrow a uterus and have what we call surrogacy.

However, the other good news is that the children produced by IVF are as normal as children born without IVF, and, in fact, in many studies they seem to be very active and intelligent individuals expressing perhaps the love and desire of their parents to have a child which seemed to be so difficult to come by.

Normal human reproduction is an inefficient process. The only reason there are so many people is that this inefficient process has twelve times a year in which it can operate. On average, only about one in four, or perhaps five meetings of sperm and egg results in a normal live birth. Occasionally, an abnormality will filter through the normal biological weeding-out process, and when this occurs we have the birth of a child with a genetic defect.

IVF technology is also inefficient because it works with a process which itself is very inefficient. IVF attempts to overcome this difficulty by transferring more than one fertilized egg. The hope is that the multiple transfers will result in a singleton birth but sometimes twins, triplets, or even high order multiple pregnancies are born. This is true not only with IVF but also of ovulation induction and ovulation enhancement, which produce very high order, multiple pregnancies.

The multiple pregnancy problem could be solved if there were some simple method to identify the in vitro fertilized egg that specifically has neonatal potential. Efforts have been made to do this from the very beginning of the in vitro process but the problem has not been solved.

Early in the IVF experience, there were attempts made to identify the oocyte that had a normal pregnancy potential. This effort was directed to examining the contents of the follicle from which particular oocytes were obtained. Examinations were made for the known hormones and other products. However, these results were never very conclusive and proved to be inefficient as a practical clinical technique. Such an effort will probably never be completely satisfactory as it ignores the contribution of the sperm. The ideal method, therefore, would be some way to test the fertilized egg that has the combination of the maternal and the paternal genetic component to determine which eggs have a normal pregnancy potential.

The first decade of the twenty-first century attempted to do just that. A major effort has used the technique of pre-implantation genetic screening, or PGS. Such a technique involves using a single cell of an eight-cell developing embryo or many more cells from a five-day embryo where a technique has been developed allowing several trophectoderm cells from the developing embryo to herniate through the egg shell or zona pellucida. This has become a standard laboratory technique. Many children have been born subsequent to this technique and there is absolutely no evidence that the technique itself—i.e., the technique of using some of the developing cells—has any adverse influence on the resulting neonates.

The PGS concept is based on the finding that a large majority—in the neighborhood of two-thirds of fertilized eggs—have an abnormality in the chromosome complement, called aneuploidy; i.e., an irregular number of chromosomes. There have been several different techniques developed to determine this aneuploidy. Furthermore, quite good results have been reported in the transfer of fertilized eggs that did not exhibit aneuploidy, that is to say the chromosome complement seemed to be normal. Some of these procedures require considerable time for the determination of the aneuploidy so that it is necessary to freeze the fertilized egg from which the biopsy has been taken to allow the patient to resume normal menstruation and transfer the previously frozen then thawed euploid; i.e., the chromosomally normal conceptus into the normally menstruating recipient. As I said, the results have been quite good based on the number of oocytes transferred.

The difficulty, however, is that the results based on the original harvested eggs is probably not greater than the ultimate pregnancy result based on the transfer of a mixture of good and bad eggs. The technique of determining aneuploidy necessarily means that fewer transfers will be done. Therefore, there will be cycles in which no transfers occur. What is happening is that it has been possible by laboratory technology to weed out at least some of those fertilized eggs where transfers occur and pregnancies do not take place. However, the process of determining aneuploidy itself results in a loss of some normal fertilized eggs. Therefore, the total number of good eggs from an egg harvest is somewhat diminished by the attempt to determine aneuploidy. Furthermore, PGS is unable to identify fertilized eggs that are incompetent due to abnormalities at the gene level. This seems to be a major category. All concerned must understand these issues. The decision to use such technology, therefore, depends on whether the patient is willing to proceed knowing these limitations. These matters are currently in the process of resolution.

A much simpler technique to determine fertilized eggs with neonatal potential lies in the examination of various compounds in the spent media in which the particular fertilized oocyte has been cultured. This technique is also being extensively studied.

One promising report has noted that the human pregnancy hormone, chorionic gonadotropin, seems to be produced very early, that is on day two as compared to later production from fertilized oocytes that do not seem to have pregnancy potential. If such a simple technique—that is the identification of a marker product such as the human pregnancy hormone—should prove to be efficient in a large number of cases, this would be a greatly simplified method of determining the fertilized egg with pregnancy potential.

A solution of this problem would be a giant step forward. It would make it possible to do single embryo transfer with great efficiency. It would make assisted reproductive technology more efficient than normal reproduction and most of all it would do away with the troubling complication of multiple pregnancies and all that that implies.

It would seem that identifying the fertilized egg with pregnancy potential would generate little bioethical or religious objection, though there may be those who would be concerned about the discard of fertilized eggs even though they were genetically abnormal. Furthermore, there is the issue of conjugal love. These are the differences between traditional religious (i.e., specifically Roman Catholic thinking) and twenty-first-century evaluation.

Preimplanation genetic diagnosis (PGD) is now a standard clinical procedure that has been in use for well over twenty years. It involves the biopsy of one of the cells of the developing conceptus. Such a cell is usually retrieved at about the eight-day cell stage, though it can be done also at the five-day stage when more than one cell can be retrieved from what is called the trophectoderm. Like PGS, there has never been any report of an infant born after PGD that seemed to be impaired by the PGD process per se. It is useful when there has been born in the family a child that is affected by what is called an autosomal recessive disorder, that is to say, a disorder caused by a contribution from both the mother and father who have carried this defective gene; or, it is sometimes used where there is a disease limited to one or the other of the sexes, usually the male. The procedure has only been used up to the present time when there has been the birth of a child that has been affected. This has indicated the use of the PGD process and there have been many normal children born as the result. The PGD process identifies the fertilized egg that is affected by the disorder in question; or, in sex-related conditions, the sex of the conceptus.

These undesirable fertilized eggs are therefore discarded.

There are some groups that object to the discarding of these fertilized eggs and have, indeed, made them available to people who wish to run the risk of raising a child affected by the disorder in question. PGD is obviously an inefficient process in that a number of the fertilized eggs will become unavailable for transfer because of their abnormality. Nevertheless, it is a highly efficient method of assuring a normal birth in the situations as described above.

Preimplantation genetic diagnosis (PGD) will surely go beyond its current ability to prevent the birth of a child with a single gene defect. With the accumulation of the monumental amount of genetic information and its association with real and potential disease traits, the time will surely come to include this information into what might be called pre-pregnancy screening or PPS. This means that it should be possible to develop a chip, indeed such chips may be in the process of being developed, which contains all those known genes of a recessive nature, which, if expressed by both partners, will result in an offspring that will have a genetic defect. Thus, it would be possible for a couple who contemplated reproduction to have a screening to determine whether there was any possibility that their child would have a double dose of the defective gene, which would give rise to a child with a genetic abnormality. In that case, they could have preimplantation genetic diagnosis before they had a child in order to determine whether they would have a fertilized egg that would be entirely normal.

The bioethical implication of this is obvious. It deals with the same problem that has been dealt with in many other occasions; namely, the recognition by contemporary information that there are normal and abnormal genetic messages in each new fertilized egg. The time has surely come to take advantage of contemporary information to improve the quality of our children. Nevertheless, there are still those who object to the discard of these abnormal fertilized eggs.

Another future development—somatic reproduction—will surely raise bioethical and religious eyebrows because it seeks to eliminate the need for donor gametes, thus eliminating the complications caused by their use both ethically and legally. Furthermore, it would assure genetic lineage as in normal reproduction for the couples seeking to reproduce. Efforts need to be made to accelerate the establishment of viable gametes from homologous somatic cells. In short, we need to pursue the road to somatic reproduction.

This would require much, much investigation. A beginning of sorts has been made when we think of the sheep, Dolly, which really was a clone from a maternal cell. In the future situation, we are speaking not of cloning but of inducing meiosis in somatic cells of the female and the somatic cells of the male. This would require much, much investigation. After this somatic meiosis has been accomplished, the cells from both partners would need to be fused and development would need to occur probably by transferring this new nucleus into an enucleated donor oocyte.

Needless to say, this would raise bioethical eyebrows, but the rewards would be tremendous. We would do away with all of the difficulties associated with donor gametes from a legal point of view and we would provide the parents with a child of genetic lineage from both parents, which is the result of normal reproduction.

An even more controversial future development is the road to exogenesis. This road was outlined by Aldoux Huxley in *Brave New World*, published in 1932. In that publication, he described IVF as science fiction. IVF has now been accomplished. He also described exogenesis, the development of the conceptus in vitro to the point of viability. This has not been accomplished in any species. Interestingly enough, in the years following the publication of *Brave New World* there were several programs around the world attempting to develop exogenesis in animals. To be sure, much animal work must be done, and, indeed, some success was achieved in the 1950s. For example, at Johns Hopkins, where I was at the time, there was a program of exogenesis among rodents that went on for many years with some success, but it was discontinued only on the retirement of the principal investigator. Research in this area has apparently been discontinued. I am unaware of any activity in this field. Nevertheless, if exogenesis could be achieved—and I feel sure that it will be sooner or later, but probably later rather than sooner—it would eliminate the necessity for surrogacy and all the social and legal complications associated with that technology.

There are other improvements in assisted reproductive technology that would probably not stir up additional bioethical or religious concerns. For example, ART in the United States produces only about 1 percent of all neonates. This is in contrast to many other countries. In Denmark, for instance, in 2007, some 5 percent of children were the result of ART. In Australia, it is around 3 percent. In many European countries, it is about 3.5 percent. Much of this is associated with the fact that national health plans provide services to cover assisted reproductive technology. This, of course, is not the case in the United States. Any moral or legal objection to this would be associated with the general concept that assisted reproductive technology in general should not be done. However, this has been much discussed in the previous sections of this book.

With the experience to date, it is difficult to understand the continued objections to the use of assisted reproductive technology, which has been most successful.

It is especially difficult to comprehend that IVF somehow or another circumvents marital love as marital love supersedes conjugal love in the experience of those who really deal with the problems of infertility and its solutions.

The marital love situation is summed up in a Mother's Day letter that Georgeanna and I sent to the children of parents who had gone the last mile in order to have them. It is as follows:

Mother's Day 1989

Dear Child,

We are the doctors who helped make it possible for you to be here. Therefore, you are very special to us and to all of those who helped us. You are our link with the supreme goal of family life—love for one another. Every child should be an expression of his or her parents' love for each other, but unfortunately this is not always so. In your case you can be sure that your mother and father love each other very dearly, as it was necessary for them to take extraordinary steps to express that love in you. You are a very special child and will grow into a very special adult because of the great love between your parents, which initiated your life and the loving care of the team of scientists who helped to make your parents' dream come true. We hope that the divine love with which you are so richly endowed will shine forth in your life, making the pathway you tread more beautiful for those who follow after you.

Howard W. Jones, Jr, M.D.

Georgeanna Seegar Jones, M.D.

The Howard and Georgeanna Jones Institute for Reproductive Medicine

# *Glossary*

| | |
|---|---|
| Abortus | A conceptus that fails to develop beyond a stage prior to birth and is discharged from the uterus. |
| AFS | American Fertility Society founded in 1944. Name changed to American Society for Reproductive Medicine (ASRM) in 1994. |
| AID | Artificial insemination donor. |
| AIH | Artificial insemination husband. |
| Andrology | The science of male reproduction. |
| ART | Assisted reproductive technology (by definition this requires the laboratory processing of the gametes from each partner). |
| ASRM | American Society for Reproductive Medicine (successor society to AFS). |
| Conceptus | A fertilized egg from fertilization to birth. |
| Ensoulment | A religious term describing the acquisition of a soul during human embryonic development. |

| | |
|---|---|
| ET | Embryo transfer—usually refers to transfer from fertilizing dish into the uterus of potential mother. |
| Human embryology | The study of human development prior to birth. |
| ICSI | Intracytoplasmic sperm injection—a laboratory technique that injects a single sperm into an egg. |
| In vitro | Literally "in a glass" (Latin); a process or reaction that occurs outside a living organism (such as in a test tube, culture dish, etc.)—opposite of *in vivo*. |
| IVF | A process by which an egg is fertilized by sperm outside the body: in vitro. Any resulting fertilized egg is then available to be transferred into the uterus of the intended mother. |
| PGD | Preimplantation genetic diagnosis—A reproductive technology used with an IVF cycle. Can be used for diagnosis of a genetic disease in early embryos prior to implantation and pregnancy. In addition, this technology can be utilized in the field of assisted reproduction for the diagnosis of unbalanced inheritance of chromosome abnormalities, such as translocations or inversions. |

| | |
|---|---|
| Personhood | A status acquired during human embryonic development that confers protection by society. |
| The Pontifical Academy of Sciences | Founded in 1603, its purpose as stated in 1989 is to inform the Vatican of progress in the mathematical, physical, and natural sciences. Organized plenary sessions and work groups eventuate in a document transmitted to the pope. |
| Preembryo | A human conceptus up to fourteen days. |
| Primagravida | A female who is pregnant for the first time. |
| Proembryo | *See* preembryo. |
| PGS | Preimplantation genetic screening. |
| Quickening | The perception of a pregnant woman of the first movement of her conceptus. |
| Spent media | Culture media after removal of a conceptus. |
| Trophectoderm | The cell layer from which the placenta arises. |

# References

"Apostolicae sedis" (*see* Pope Pius IX, 1869).

American Fertility Society Ethics Committee.

————1986. Ethical considerations of the new reproductive technologies. *Fertil Steril* 46(3) Suppl 1.

————. 1986. New guidelines for the use of semen for donor insemination. *Fertil Steril* 46(2) Suppl 2

————. 1988. Ethical considerations of the new reproductive technologies in the light of *Instruction on respect for human life in its origin and on the dignity of procreation* issued by the Congregation for the Doctrine of Faith. *Fertil Steril* 49(2) Suppl 1.

————. 1990. Ethical considerations of the new reproductive technologies: Ethics Committee of The American Fertility Society. *Fertil Steril* 53(6) Suppl 2.

————. 1994. Ethics Committee of the American Fertility Society, The Biologic Characteristics of the preembryo: Ethical considerations of assisted reproductive technologies. Fertil Steril 62 (Suppl 1)

Aristotle. 350 BCE. Book VII. *The History of Animals.* [Classics] Greece.

————. *De Anima.* [Classics] Greece.

Benagiano G, GC Di Renzo, EV Cosmi E, JD Woods, and E Mordini, eds. 1996. *The evolution of the meaning of sexual intercourse in the human.* Firenze, Italy: International Institute for the Study of Man. [From the international meeting on "The evolution of the meaning of sexual intercourse in the human" held in Caprarola, Italy, 19–21 October 1992.]

Blackstone, William (1979) [1765]. Amendment IX, Doc 1. *Commentaries on the Laws of England*. Chicago: University of Chicago Press.

Canada. Parliament. 1869. *Criminal Code of Canada* [since overturned].

Chang, MC. 1959. Fertilization of rabbit ova *in vitro*. *Nature* 184:466.

Cicero, Marcus Tullius (106–43 BCE). In Defence of Cluentius. [Classics] Rome.

Congregation for the Doctrine of the Faith. 1987. Instruction *Donum vitae* on respect for human life in its origin and on the dignity of procreation. Vatican AAS 80 (1988).

———. 2008. Instruction *Dignitas personae* on certain bioethical questions. Vatican website www.vatican.va/romancuria/congregations/cfaith/documents/rcconcfaithdoc20081208dignitas-personaeen.html [accessed 2012]

Crockin, SL and HW Jones, Jr. 2000. *See* entry under Jones.

———. 2009. *Legal conceptions: the evolving law and policy of assisted reproductive technologies*. Baltimore: The Johns Hopkins University Press.

*Davis v. Davis*. 1989. September 21. No. E-14496, WL 140495 (Tenn. Cir. Ct. Sept. 21).

———. 1992. 842 S.W. 2d 588, 597 (Tenn.)

Ebers Papyrus. c 1550 BCE. [Classics] Egypt. [The text in English translation: Ebbell, B., ed. *The Papyrus Ebers*. Copenhagen: Munksgaard, 1937.]

Edwards RG and P Steptoe. 1980. *A matter of life*. London: Hutchinson & Co.

————, RP Donahue, TA Baramki, and HW Jones, Jr. 1966. Preliminary attempts to fertilize human oocytes matured in vitro. *Am J Obstet Gynecol* 96:192.

*Effraenatam* (*see* Pope Sixtus V, 1588).

*Evangelium vitae* (*see* Pope John II).*Gaudium et spes* (*see* Pope Paul VI, 1965).

Goodman, MF. 1988. *What is a person?* Humana Press, Clifton, NJ, 1988.

Gratian. Ca. 1140. *Decretum Gratiani*.

*Griswald v. Connecticut*. 1965. U.S. Supreme Court. 381 U.S. 479. [Held that birth control was protected by "a right to privacy."]

Grobstein, Clifford. 1984, August 8–9. "Eight points to establish a suitable deliberating mechanism for the whole range of new reproductive options." Hearing before the Subcommittee on Investigations and Oversights of the Committee on Science and Technology of the House of Representatives, Chairman Al Gore (rep. Tennessee). Washington, DC.

Hammurabi. c 1700 BCE. *Code of Hammurabi*. [Classics] Babylonia. [Visit the Yale Law School website for a text translation: http://avalon.law.yale.edu/ancient/hamframe.asp]

Henle, Robert J. 1971. Bioethics center formed. *Chem Eng News*. 49(42):7.

Huser J. 1942. *The crime of abortion in canon law: An historical synopsis and commentary*. The Catholic University of America Press.

Hayashi Y, M Saitou, and S Yamanaka. 2012. Germline development from human pluripotent stem cells toward disease modeling of infertility. *Fertil Steril* 97:1250.

*Humanae vitae* (*see* Pope Paul VI, 1968).

Huxley A. 1932. *Brave new world.* London: Chatto & Windus.

*Johnson v. Calvert.* 1993. 5 Cal. 4th 84, 851 P.2d 776. 19 Cal. Rptr. 2d 494.

Jones GS. 1987. Reply to the Vatican *Instruction on respect for human life in its origin and on the dignity of procreation.* Vol. 2, No. 3 of *Fertility News.*

Jones HW. 1984. Prepared statement. Hearing before the Subcommittee on Investigations and Oversights of the Committee on Science and Technology of the House of Representatives. [*Also see* Grobstein]

Jones HW and J Cohen, eds. 1999. IFFS surveillance 98. *Fertil Steril* 71(5) Suppl 2.

———. 2001. IFFS surveillance 01. *Fertil Steril* 76(5) Suppl 2.

———. 2004. IFFS surveillance 04. *Fertil Steril* 81(5) Suppl 4.

———. 2007. IFFS surveillance 07. *Fertil Steril* 87(4) Suppl 1.

Jones HW, I Cooke, R Kempers, P Brinsden, and D Saunders, eds. 2011. IFFS surveillance 2010. *Fertil Steril* 95(2).

Jones HW and S Crockin. 2000. On assisted reproduction, religion and civil law. *Fertil Steril:* 73(3).

Jones HW and C Schrader. 1989. And just what is a pre-embryo? *Fertil Steril* 52:189.

Kass LR. 1971. Babies by means of in vitro fertilization: unethical experiments on the unborn? *N Engl J Med* 285(21):1174.

Kushner T. 1984. Having a life versus being alive. *J Med Ethics* 10:5.

*Ledger-Star, The.* 1979. Both sides swap barbs over test-tube babies. November 1. Norfolk, VA.

Miller J and B Brubaker. 1990. *Bioethics and the beginning of life: An Anabaptist perspective.* Scottdale, PA: Herald Press.

Pope Benedict XVI. 2010. *See* Tertullian.

Pope John II. 1995. *Evangelium vitae.* Città del Vaticano: Libreria Editrice Vaticana [Text accessed 2012: www.vatican.va/holy_father/john_paul_ii/encyclicals/documents/hf_jp-ii_enc_25031995_evangelium-vitae_en.html]

Pope John Paul II. 1994. *Crossing the threshold of hope.* New York: Knopf.

Pope Paul VI. 1966. Pastoral constitution on the church in the modern world *Gaudium et spes.*

Pope Pius IX. 1869. Papal bull Apostolicae sedis. *Actae sanctae sedis.* Vatican.

Pope Sixtus V. 1588. Papal bull *Effraenatam.* Rome: Vatican.

Ramsey P. 1972. Shall we "reproduce"? I. The medical ethics of in vitro fertilization. *JAMA* 220(10):1346. [Speech before the International Symposium on Human Rights, Retardation, and Research, sponsored by the Joseph P. Kennedy, Jr., Foundation, in Washington, DC, Oct 16, 1971.]

———. 1972. Shall we "reproduce"? II. Rejoinders and future forecast. *JAMA* 220(11):1480. [Speech before the International Symposium on Human Rights . . . DC, 1971.]

Rimm AA, AC Katayama, and KP Katayama. 2011. A meta-analysis of the impact of IVF and ICSI on major malformations after adjusting for the effect of subfertility. *J Assist Reprod Genet* 28:699.

*Roe v. Wade.* 1973. Supreme Court. 410 U.S. 113.

United Kingdom. House of Commons. 1861. *Offenses Against the Person Act.* [Outlaws abortion.]

U.S. Congress. 1873. *Comstock Act.* [Hist. Dclrd unconstitutional in 1983.]

———. House. 1992 *Fertility Clinic Success Rate and Certification Act of 1992.* HR 4773ENR. 102nd Cong. (1991–1992). *Congressional Record* pub L, no. 102–493.

Vatican. Cathecism of the Catholic Church. Website source: www.vatican.va/archive/ccc_css/archive/catechism/p1s2c1p6.htm [accessed 2012].

Veeck LL and N Zaninovic. 2003. *An atlas of human blastocysts.* London: Parthenon.

Veeck LL. 1986. *An atlas of the human oocyte and early conceptus.* Vol. I. Baltimore: Williams & Wilkins.

———1999. *An atlas of human gametes and conceptuses.* London: Parthenon.

———. 1991. *An atlas of the human oocyte and early conceptus.* Vol. II. Baltimore: Williams & Wilkins.

*Virginian Pilot, The.* 1982. Doctors sue Landmark for libel. December 9. Norfolk, VA.

Wyden, Ron. 1992. Fertility Clinic Success Rate and Certification Act (proposed). Pub. L. 102-493, 42 U.S.C. 263a-1 et seq. HR 4773ENR, 102nd Cong (1991–1992).

*York v. Jones.* 1989. 717 F. Supp. 421. [The Norfolk program was sued in the Federal Circuit Court over possession of cryopreserved fertilized egg.]

# *About the Author*

Howard W. Jones, Jr., was born in Baltimore, Maryland, on December 30, 1910. He received his A.B. in 1931 from Amherst College and his M.D. in 1935 from the Johns Hopkins University School of Medicine. Because of age, he was required to retire from Johns Hopkins in 1978 and was appointed professor of obstetrics and gynecology at the Eastern Virginia Medical School, where he and his wife, Georgeanna Seegar Jones, established the first in vitro fertilization program in the United States.